BACKROADS & BYWAYS OF

CHESAPEAKE BAY

BACKROADS & BYWAYS OF

CHESAPEAKE BAY

*Drives, Day Trips &
Weekend Excursions*

SECOND EDITION

LESLIE ATKINS

THE COUNTRYMAN PRESS

A division of W. W. Norton & Company

Independent Publishers Since 1923

We welcome your comments and suggestions. Please contact:
Editor
The Countryman Press
500 Fifth Avenue
New York, NY 10110
or e-mail countrymanpress@wwnorton.com

Copyright © 2020, 2014 by LA Communications, LLC
Maps by Michael Borop, siteatlas.com © The Countryman Press
All photographs by Leslie Atkins unless otherwise specified.

For information about permission to reproduce selections from this book, write to
Permissions, The Countryman Press, 500 Fifth Avenue, New York, NY 10110

For information about special discounts for bulk purchases, please contact
W. W. Norton Special Sales at specialsales@wwnorton.com or 800-233-4830

Manufacturing by Versa Press
Series book design by Chris Welch
The Countryman Press
www.countrymanpress.com

A division of W. W. Norton & Company, Inc.
500 Fifth Avenue, New York, NY 10110
www.wwnorton.com

978-1-68268-432-0 (pbk.)

10 9 8 7 6 5 4 3 2 1

To my dad, who shared with me his love of books and writing.
He loved me unconditionally and I know he'd be proud.
To my mom, who was always curious and interested in exploring.
She doted on me and loved me with all her heart.
Both taught me warmth and the true value of good conversation
in getting to know people and the places they enjoy most.

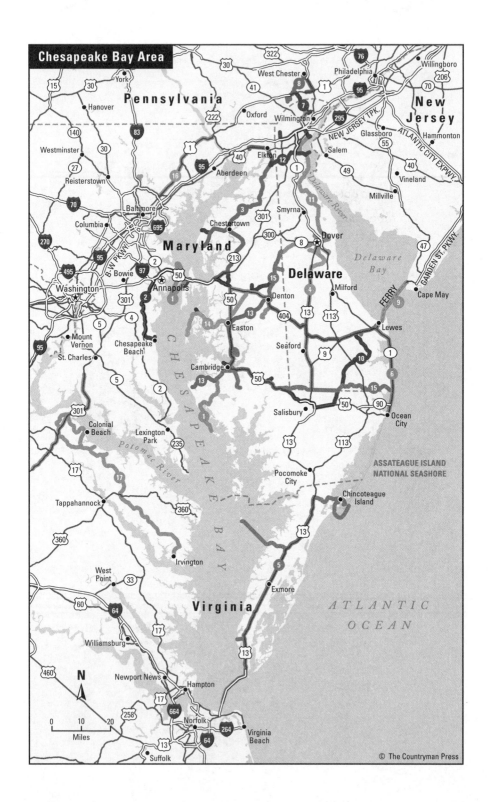

Contents

Introduction

*Sail away from the safe harbor. Catch the trade winds in your sails. Explore.
Dream. Discover.* —Mark Twain

The land between the Chesapeake and Delaware Bays is all about extensive coastlines and the wonders they bring. The waters are vital to defending those coasts and protecting everything onshore. It's thrilling to reap the joy and sustenance provided by the waters and to revel in the abundant beauty all around.

The Delmarva Peninsula—with parts in Delaware, Maryland, and Virginia—is a unique region with a distinct personality formed by a mixture of exuberance and practicality.

First settled by Native Americans from the Nanticoke and Choptank tribes among others, the region later became home to Dutch and English settlers. Remnants of names and agricultural products from the Native Americans tell part of the tale.

Artistic and architectural creations in the European model tell another. The region's history creates context; there is a powerful connection between where the region is now, what came before, and what is yet to come.

When I set out to create this guide, I began with Delaware and the Maryland Eastern Shore. The more I researched, the more it became apparent state boundaries matter little when you're in the Brandywine Valley crossing from Delaware into Pennsylvania to view more art and gardens, or on the Cape May–Lewes Ferry heading to Cape May, New Jersey.

Likewise, borderlines matter little when you're out on the Chesapeake Bay about to leave Maryland waters to set foot on the Virginia soil of Tangier Island.

It does not matter whether the fresh rockfish on your plate was caught in the Chesapeake Bay or in one of the rivers that feed it, or if it was caught in the Delaware Bay.

And it is rather unimportant whether you happen to see a beautiful heron at the rookery on Pea Patch Island in the Delaware River or in the Maryland marshes of Smith Island. Whether you're relaxing at a waterfront crab house in Delaware or on Maryland's Eastern Shore—it's all good.

New Jersey's Cape May is on the Atlantic Ocean. Also on the Atlantic are the beaches in Southern Delaware; in Ocean City, Maryland; and along miles of Virginia's Eastern Shore, which are separated from mainland Virginia by about 17 miles of water. They're all wonderful, all interconnected, all of a piece.

These places make up part of a beautiful picture, a delicious taste of nature at its best, a charming section of the East Coast just begging travelers to enjoy its bounty—from delicious seafood to pirate treasure spit up by waves during a storm, a storm not unlike the ones that probably sank the pirate vessels back in the day.

Perhaps the best part of this voyage through the region is that you're never far away from water—ocean, rivers, streams, creeks, and bays: the wonderful Chesapeake and Delaware Bays. Somehow the ever-present water is a blending factor, mixing nature and civilization, culture and commerce, even the past, present, and future—all bound together in beauty, in continuity, and in a pleasurable way of life, whether for a day, a weekend, or a lifetime.

The bays are estuaries—large, partially enclosed bodies of water where freshwater from rivers and streams mixes with salt water from the ocean. At different places in an estuary, this mixture varies, thus providing the bedrock for varied species of plants, fish, and other wildlife.

REPLICA OF AN INDIAN LONGHOUSE

SANDY POINT SHOAL LIGHT

The Chesapeake Bay is the largest estuary in the United States, with about half its water volume coming from its enormous river watershed and the other half from the Atlantic Ocean. Smaller but still vital, the Delaware Bay is an outlet of the Delaware River, also mixing with the salt water of the Atlantic.

Rivers and creeks often seem interchangeable in size, depending on where they are located. And the ocean looms as a leviathan, with its major impact on the bays and on the entire region.

Whether you're off on a spontaneous excursion, a last-minute getaway, or a planned trip, keeping this book on the dining room table or tucked into the front seat of the car will help expedite your journey.

Consider keeping an overnight bag packed and secured in the trunk of the car, just in case. Perhaps you'll decide, on the spur of the moment, to stop and take a hike or to hole up in a B&B for the night. A pair of Nikes and sweats, or jeans and a jacket, plus the indispensable toothbrush, can come in pretty handy.

Travel, whether you are coming from far away or exploring in your relative backyard, means leaving your own sphere and arriving at a new, unknown place. An excursion is an exciting adventure, wherever you go. It's certainly an antidote to stress and hard work, and a way to experience enticing places and intriguing pursuits. Often it triggers memories of long-ago travel or creates new ones to be enjoyed in coming years. It certainly moves us in unanticipated and wondrous ways, leaving us different than when we started.

With a sailboat and a favorable wind, or a car and a full tank of gas on a sunny day, you're likely to find the desire to travel irresistible.

I spent a lot of time looking for unique and appealing places and activities to recommend. I sincerely hope my ideas and observations help foster your own personal adventures throughout the region flanked by the Delaware and Chesapeake Bays and touched by the Atlantic Ocean to the south and the Brandywine Valley to the north.

Many who cross the Chesapeake Bay Bridge or come from Norfolk across the Chesapeake Bay Bridge–Tunnel will smell salt water in their imaginations and single-mindedly head for the beach. While that's wonderful, there are many other places to visit once you're on and near the Delmarva Peninsula.

Many places are covered in this book, but it's virtually impossible to include every nook and cranny in such a large region. Follow the paths described here, but also take side trips on your own. Discovery, after all, is always exciting.

You can also cut and paste the excursions to create new journeys, incorporating part of one itinerary and part of another—to mix and match the adventures, as it were.

Whether you call it getting off the grid, traveling back roads, staying off the beaten path, exploring outside the box, or avoiding tourists and the touristy places that cater to them, the aim of this book is to reveal interesting, beautiful, appealing, and relaxing things to do and places to see—nearby and yet not well-known—and to encourage you to go beyond the obvious.

To make each journey more pleasurable, plan to avoid crossing onto the peninsula on a Friday afternoon or leaving on a Sunday night during the summer, at least if you have another alternative, in order to avoid the crowds and incumbent delays.

Often it is little roadblocks and annoyances that make some of the best memories. You just want to keep them small and infrequent.

I hope this book will assist you in the quest for memorable but relaxing and stimulating journeys. It helps to keep in mind that the journey is as important as the destination, while you seek to find your own unique travel rhythm. That's what meandering is all about.

I want to send a huge thank-you to the wonderful people at The Countryman Press and W. W. Norton who gave me an excuse to further explore the Mid-Atlantic region in creating this book. Not that I needed an excuse, for I love travel and also love the waterways and the land between the waters throughout the Chesapeake region. To everyone who lovingly assisted in the development of this book, I am forever grateful.

Practical Stuff

PACKING FOR THE ROAD

The usual tendency for most of us is to pack too much when we're traveling by car. After all, there are no weight or baggage restrictions like those imposed by the airlines. And you're not carrying bags through a train or bus terminal.

However, it is advisable to resist the temptation to overpack, for going light is as much a state of mind as it is a reality. Following a long day spent in the car, you'll want a small, lightweight bag to carry up the steps in a B&B or when you check into your room at a hotel.

After all, you still have to lift the bag in and out of the trunk, even if it's on wheels. And the less baggage you carry, the more open you are to new places and experiences. You want to avoid stuffing the car full of luggage, food, and other assorted clutter.

Of course, you may need a spare pair of sneakers if yours get wet while you're walking in the dunes after a rain. Or you may need a warm jacket to go out on a boat. If these situations are likely, pack a separate bag for such contingencies and leave it in your car when you go into your accommodations for the night. The extra items will be there if you need them; either way, your overnight bag will be light and freeing.

Inside your car or truck, you'll no doubt want certain gadgets—GPS, a phone charger for the car (you'll also want a regular one in your overnight bag), a tire pressure gauge, and an extra pack of tire valve caps. Always keep a flashlight and a blanket in the car for emergencies, plus this book, of course, whether in hard copy or as an e-book.

Packing a small cooler with cold drinks and bottles of water, plus some high-energy snacks like nuts or raisins, is a good idea.

If you're traveling with someone who has different temperature

Happiness is a journey, not a destination.

FLOWERS AND WISDOM, INN AT MONTCHANIN VILLAGE

preferences from you, one or both of you might want to leave a sweater or light jacket in the car.

You might want to pack a separate beach bag if you plan to go swimming. Include a beach towel, flip-flops, bathing suit and cover-up, suntan lotion, sunglasses, a hat, and bug spray.

It may sound as though you're taking even more stuff, but the trick is organization: small separate bags for different purposes (overnight, in the car, on the beach).

Whatever you decide to leave at home, bring at least one digital camera, a battery charger and extra memory card (or a smartphone with a superb built-in camera). Keep the camera handy, for you never know when a family of ducks will waddle across the road on Chincoteague Island or a dolphin will pop its nose up out of the water in front of the Cape May–Lewes Ferry as it crosses Delaware Bay.

MOVING AROUND

Most of these itineraries include plenty of stops along the way. If you find yourself driving a long distance at one time—perhaps to get to a starting point or to head home—stop somewhere safe every few hours to stretch and move around, and let your passengers do so too. Being on the road will be that much more enjoyable.

WEATHER

Most of the roads in this book are in coastal areas. Heavy rains can bring flooding, especially in places near sea level. Your weekend plans can easily get washed away, but better your plans wash away than you and your car.

Always be aware of the weather report when traveling in this region, and

FAMILY OF DUCKS ON CHINCOTEAGUE

talk to locals about roads that may be flooded. Remember the rule for flooded roadways: Do not drive in standing or moving water. Back up if necessary.

Overall, it's best to avoid driving when the weather is problematic. Consider staying on at your lodging an extra day, especially if conditions preclude getting home safely. If meteorologists are warning of imminent problems, think about postponing your trip altogether, even at the last minute.

GAS TANK

It's best to keep the gas tank full when you're driving these routes. In many places, there are plenty of gas stations, but you can get caught in other spots without options. Play it safe and always fill up when you have the chance, which is less stressful than worrying you might run out of gas on a deserted stretch.

Geographic Designations

While visiting Easton, Maryland, I happened to have a discussion over breakfast with a lovely husband and wife who were enjoying a sojourn in the area. They have lived and traveled around the world, but they are entranced by this region and the interesting places to see.

The wife was originally from Alabama, and she casually asked me what constitutes the Eastern Shore. As a native Marylander, I am naturally familiar with the state, and I've traveled it extensively to research the trips I recommend.

From her question, it immediately became apparent to me that readers from farther away might need some definitions. Thus, this section evolved to define a few important geographic designations.

EASTERN SHORE

I imagine there are other Eastern Shores in the United States, no doubt bordering various lakes and rivers. However, in the Mid-Atlantic region, the Chesapeake Bay is prominent and vital—economically, militarily, culturally, and recreationally. Here "Eastern Shore" generally refers to all of Maryland east of the Chesapeake Bay, from Elkton in the north to Pocomoke City and Crisfield in the south, and from Kent Island in the west to Ocean City and Assateague Island in the east.

What many people forget, or perhaps don't know, is that there's also a contiguous peninsula south of the Maryland Eastern Shore that belongs to Virginia. This is the Virginia Eastern Shore, which extends to Cape Charles at the meeting point of the Chesapeake Bay and the Atlantic Ocean.

WESTERN SHORE

People who live on Maryland's "Western Shore" don't generally think of it that way. It's obvious if you look at a map that the Chesapeake Bay cuts the state practically in two. But to those who live in Baltimore, the suburbs of Washington, DC, Annapolis, Columbia, Havre de Grace, Southern Maryland, or Western Maryland, there's the Eastern Shore and then there's the rest of Maryland.

However, if you live on the Eastern Shore, there's life on the water and then there's life on the other side—the Western Shore, the one you reach when you cross "the bridge," referring to the Chesapeake Bay Bridge.

There's also a large tract of land in Virginia replete with many waterways; this land lies on the western side of the Chesapeake Bay and extends from the Potomac River to Norfolk. The area comprises what locals call the Northern Neck, Middle Peninsula, and Virginia or Lower Peninsula. The geographic term "neck" refers to a long, thin peninsula that resembles a neck-like area on a map.

These Virginia peninsulas are largely defined by their shoreline with the bay as well as the paths of the Potomac, Rappahannock, York, and James rivers flowing into the Chesapeake.

TOLLBOOTH TO THE BRIDGE-TUNNEL BETWEEN NORFOLK AND VIRGINIA EASTERN SHORE

DELMARVA PENINSULA

"Delmarva" is an abbreviation coined about a century ago to represent all of DELaware, the Eastern Shore of MARyland, and the Eastern Shore of VirginiA—the peninsula traveled in this book.

I've included the Brandywine Valley extension into Pennsylvania because part of the valley is in Delaware. The beach town of Cape May, New Jersey, is also part of this journey since the ferry that travels across the Delaware Bay from the town of Lewes, Delaware, to Cape May is a major part of exploring Southern Delaware. I've also added in aspects of Maryland in and around Baltimore and a visit to Virginia's Northern Neck, for the Chesapeake Bay influences both shores. As I said in the introduction, state lines don't seem to apply when it comes to this special peninsula, situated as it is between two large bays—the Chesapeake and the Delaware—and edged with a large Atlantic shoreline.

The Delmarva Peninsula is the second-largest peninsula in the eastern United States; Florida is the largest.

Brandywine Valley

The Brandywine River begins in Pennsylvania and runs into the Delaware River, which then runs into the Delaware Bay before heading out to the Atlantic Ocean. The Brandywine Valley is a beautiful area situated around the river of the same name. The entire valley is resplendent with lovely vistas that have long inspired artists and landowners.

From industrialists to artists, and from wealthy landowners to conservationists, people have sought to capture the beauty of the valley in art, grand estates, mansions, and world-famous gardens.

The valley itself runs from the southeastern corner of Pennsylvania into northern Delaware. Often referred to as "chateau country" due to its grand French-style estates, it begins about 30 miles southwest of Philadelphia and stretches 10 or 11 miles into Delaware, to Wilmington.

This scenic valley is the home and bastion of the Du Pont industrial dynasty in America. It also gave rise to the dynasty of artists with the last name of Wyeth, including illustrator N. C. Wyeth, as well as his son Andrew Wyeth and his grandson Jamie Wyeth.

The Brandywine Valley is magnificent with fertile land and country charm. Towns of note include Chadds Ford, Kennett Square, and West Chester in Pennsylvania, and Middletown, Montchanin, New Castle, Port Penn, and Newark in Delaware.

Wilmington and the Brandywine Valley are within a three-hour drive of a third of the US population. By car, I-95 ties the area to New York, Philadelphia, Baltimore, and Washington, DC.

ASSATEAGUE AND CHINCOTEAGUE ISLANDS

The geography around these two islands can be a bit confusing, even after you've been there, so here's the scoop. Assateague Island is a barrier island in the Atlantic Ocean, partially on Maryland's Eastern Shore and partially on Virginia's Eastern Shore. A barrier island is a narrow coastal strip of land parallel to the mainland.

Assateague Island is approximately 38 miles long, with about two-thirds of the island in Maryland and the other third in Virginia. In the Maryland portion, a small percentage of the land is a state park, while the larger percentage is part of Assateague Island National Seashore.

In the Virginia portion, the northern section is a continuation of Assateague Island National Seashore. The southern end is the Chincoteague National Wildlife Refuge (CNWR).

Chincoteague Island is another barrier island just west of Virginia's portion of Assateague Island. Chincoteague is protected from the Atlantic Ocean by Assateague Island, and it is just across from Assateague via a short bridge over Assateague Channel.

BIRDS IN CHINCOTEAGUE NATIONAL WILDLIFE REFUGE

To reach Chincoteague Island, motorists travel several miles across a dramatic causeway through wetlands and marshes and then across a drawbridge onto the island.

Assateague (in Maryland) and Chincoteague are each known for having a herd of wild ponies. The Chincoteague ponies actually live on Assateague Island in the CNWR. The two herds are kept separate by a fence along the Virginia-Maryland border on the island.

You can drive on the Maryland portion of Assateague via access close to Ocean City. You can also drive on the Virginia portion. However, there is no road that runs the entire length of the island.

On Getting Lost

As a little girl growing up in Baltimore, my life was good. However, it was with some trepidation that I approached Sundays. That was the day before my weekend homework was due, and I invariably procrastinated. That was also the day my father usually took my mother, brother, and me for a long drive in the family car.

Mom always wanted to have a destination, but Dad enjoyed the process of the journey and didn't need one. Sitting in the backseat, my brother and I listened to this debate each week, while I worried about getting home late because of homework left to do, and I also worried about our getting lost.

Little did I know at age seven, eight, or nine that home was where the family was, whether we knew the location or not. After all, my days of being a philosopher and writer were yet to come.

Only now, years later, do I understand that my parents always knew they could find a road that would lead home. They also knew they could trust themselves and, perhaps more importantly, they knew they could trust each other.

My parents shared with us their spirit of exploration. Those car trips were vitally important, for they were outings during which we talked, listened to the same music, and played games like watching for unusual mailboxes or counting the number of states we would find on license plates of passing cars—special Sunday things that created family memories more precious than diamonds, now that the past is gone.

I no longer worry about getting lost. In fact, now I love it when that happens. Inevitably I discover some hole-in-the-wall country store or a back road with a beautiful view of farmland or an interesting riverbank.

And I trust that I will find my way home, eventually.

WHIMSICAL MAILBOX ON HOOPER ISLAND

1

VIEWING LIGHTHOUSES IN THE CHESAPEAKE

ESTIMATED LENGTH: 270 miles, plus various nautical miles on the bay

ESTIMATED TIME: 3 days

GETTING THERE: From the Chesapeake Bay Bridge, take US 50 East. Take the first exit after the bridge, exit 37, onto MD 8. At the top of the ramp, bear right onto Romancoke Road. Turn right at the first light onto Pier One Road and park at Hemingway's Restaurant next to Bay Bridge Marina. After the boat tour, get back on US 50 East. Before reaching the town of Easton, turn right onto the Easton Bypass, MD 322. Travel 2 miles and turn right again onto MD 33 (St. Michaels Road) to the town of St. Michaels.

HIGHLIGHTS: Boat tour of several original Chesapeake Bay lighthouses from Stevensville; drive onto Tilghman Island, eating steamed blue crabs; Chesapeake Bay Maritime Museum; boating underneath the Chesapeake Bay Bridge; driving tour of lighthouses from St. Michaels to Cambridge to Hooper Island; charming isolation on Hooper Island.

LIGHTHOUSES ON THE BAY

Although the era of lighthouse culture and mystique has faded, the "lights"—as they are known—still draw our attention, just as ship captains have long been attracted by their protective beacons.

How to go about visiting the lighthouses on the Chesapeake and Delaware Bays is a multilayered decision, depending on which ones you want to see. Some are visible from shore, while others can only be reached by

TILGHMAN ISLAND PIER

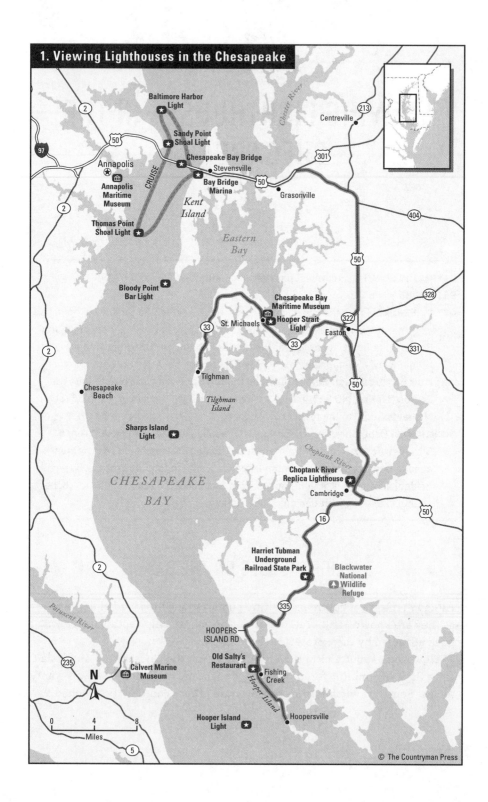

1. Viewing Lighthouses in the Chesapeake

Baltimore Harbor Light

Sandy Point Shoal Light

Chesapeake Bay Bridge

Stevensville

Bay Bridge Marina

Grasonville

Annapolis

Annapolis Maritime Museum

CRUISE

Kent Island

Thomas Point Shoal Light

Centreville

Eastern Bay

Bloody Point Bar Light

Chesapeake Bay Maritime Museum

St. Michaels

Hooper Strait Light

Easton

Tilghman

Tilghman Island

Chesapeake Beach

Sharps Island Light

CHESAPEAKE BAY

Choptank River

Choptank River Replica Lighthouse

Cambridge

Harriet Tubman Underground Railroad State Park

Blackwater National Wildlife Refuge

Patuxent River

HOOPERS ISLAND RD

Old Salty's Restaurant

Fishing Creek

Hooper Island

Calvert Marine Museum

N

Hooper Island Light

Hoopersville

0   4   8

Miles

© The Countryman Press

boat. You can't do them all in one day, but you can do them all, either on an extended visit or a series of trips.

In this journey, we'll focus on lights in and around the middle portion of the Chesapeake Bay that are reachable or visible from the Maryland Eastern Shore, including six offshore lights and two on land. This is by no means all of them, but it's a great start and a wonderful way to gain a true sense of lighthouses and their importance in maritime history.

Many of the other lights are on Maryland's Western Shore, as well as a few along Virginia's Western Shore. Some, including ones in Delaware, in Cape May, New Jersey, and on Virginia's Eastern Shore, will be seen in other journeys outlined elsewhere in this book.

Lighthouses are symbols of the past, before radar, GPS, and satellite transmissions made them mostly technologically obsolete.

They remain along the Mid-Atlantic shore, some rusting into oblivion and others lovingly restored by romantics determined to maintain the lore of the sea from a time when the lights guided loved ones home. Only a few are still in use for navigation.

The lights each have their own special allure, with stories of disaster and near-disaster. There's romance that surrounds these structures too, with tales of seafarers, lighthouse keepers, and even ghosts.

Thus, while technology advances, these endangered historic landmarks continue to have their place.

Those who love the lights can take all-day group tours given by private charter captains and by **Calvert Marine Museum** on Solomons Island off

CHESAPEAKE BAY MARITIME MUSEUM ON MILES RIVER IN ST. MICHAELS

the Western Shore. The **Annapolis Maritime Museum**, also on the Western Shore, sponsors short trips to one lighthouse—**Thomas Point Shoal Light**.

Or you can charter a boat through one of the captains with **Watermen Heritage Tours** and just visit some of the more interesting lighthouses. If you do the latter, you can go island-hopping at the same time, visiting a treasure like Smith Island or Tangier Island in the Chesapeake for a crabcake lunch.

Be prepared to hear stories about the ravages of storms, fires, and ice floes—all of which have taken their toll on a number of lighthouses.

There are also tales of wives who took up the keeping of the lights upon the deaths of their husbands—quite an isolated yet important function for these women used to living in a lighthouse.

Several of the lighthouses are onshore, so we'll follow a driving route to visit some of them later. Others are offshore on tiny bits of land that in some cases were larger sections of land that have eroded away, leaving the lighthouses out in the middle of the bay by themselves.

To reach the offshore lighthouses, you'll need to go out in a boat. Perhaps the most well-known tour company is **Chesapeake Lighthouses** out of **Stevensville**, which is just past the **Chesapeake Bay Bridge** on the Maryland Eastern Shore.

Plan to arrive the night before your boat tour, especially if it's summertime, when it can be tricky to get through traffic crossing the Bay Bridge.

FORMER STEVENSVILLE TRAIN DEPOT

And stay over afterward to visit some of the lights accessible by car. A lovely option is to check in at the **Inn at Perry Cabin** in **St. Michaels** or in **Easton** at **Tidewater Inn.**

You can have dinner at the one of the inns or try one of the many excellent restaurants nearby. A good choice in St. Michaels for delicious pizza or pasta is **Ava's Pizzeria & Wine Bar**, or in **Easton**, try the friendly **Out of the Fire.** Then relax, for tomorrow will be a pleasant day out on the Chesapeake.

On the boat. For this trip, we'll take the two-hour, three-light daytime "Triangle" tour with Chesapeake Lighthouses. (Participants often joke about the three-hour tour that sparked the plot for *Gilligan's Island.*)

From the parking lot at **Hemingway's Restaurant**, find your way down the street to **Bay Bridge Marina** and the boat named *Sharps Island.* It's a good idea to make advance reservations, but you can often book at the last minute for trips Thursday through Sunday during the months of June to November.

Once on board, the captain reviews safety precautions before leaving the dock. The boat is Coast Guard approved, and the captain's experience is reassuring.

Just in case there's a problem, life preservers are in clear view. The captain explains that he'll say "Clamp on" if the boat hits a wave; this means everyone should hold on to a railing or rope. In poor weather conditions, everyone will be instructed to leave the front of the boat and take cover in the back. Safety first, of course, but with that out of the way, the journey begins.

There's nothing like being out on the Chesapeake Bay on a pretty summer afternoon. It's peaceful and relaxing, a chance to get out of your car and see these fascinating remnants of a time gone by in boating and shipping, before GPS and other advanced navigation tools. Yet even today, some of the lights mark shoals and serve as "site marks." (They can't be landmarks because they're either in the water or on a tiny bit of land surrounded by water.)

The order of the boat tour's itinerary varies based on the captain's mood, sea conditions, or special events in the area. For instance, on a day when there's a swimming or boating event, the tour may vary to avoid the other activities. But the same three lights are always covered—**Thomas Point**, **Sandy Point**, and **Baltimore Harbor Light.** The boat holds 29 passengers, but the captain generally limits each tour to 18 people to allow extra room so everyone is comfortable.

For your personal comfort, it helps to plan ahead by bringing certain items with you when you're out on the water. These include a windbreaker, a warm hat, a camera or smartphone with a good built-in camera, comfortable nonskid soft-soled shoes, sunscreen, sunglasses, lunch, water, and snacks. You can pick up lunch at the **Love Point Deli** in **Stevensville,** not far from Bay Bridge Marina, where the boat is docked.

Steamed Crabs

After several hours driving along backroads or boating on the bay, sitting down to the communal activity of eating steamed blue crabs is a natural. This activity is bred into the DNA of Marylanders, as well as some who grew up in parts of Virginia and Delaware. To outsiders, it is likely to seem strange. Therefore, a bit of an education is in order.

First, crabs are prevalent in Mid-Atlantic waters. One should eat them with enthusiasm but also caution. A bad one can make you sick, and eating the "devil" (the gray featherlike stuff underneath the outer shell) can definitely make you ill. Steamed crabs are expensive, ranging up to $120 or more a dozen in some restaurants, so no one wants to discard any. However, if the taste is off or the crab doesn't seem right, it's standard to send it back for a replacement. Don't mess with a bad crab.

Similarly, if you find a dead or sluggish crab on the beach, you shouldn't steam it—you should pitch it. Instead you want to eat blue crabs caught by crabbers in nets or in crab pots near the shore or a dock, as well as in the center of the bay.

Blue crabs are steamed live, similar to the handling of lobsters as immortalized in the lobster-wrangling scene from Woody Allen's film *Annie Hall*, where the lobsters run around, trying to stay out of the pot. Crabs don't usually run around, but it is common to hear them trying to get out of the pot.

Obviously, this doesn't seem too pleasant for the crabs. However, sitting with other people and eating the delectable steamed crabs covered with Old Bay Seasoning is a highly social activity.

A CRABCAKE FOR THOSE WHO WANT CRABMEAT ALREADY OUT OF THE SHELL

STEAMED BLUE CRABS WITH OLD BAY SEASONING

Second, it takes time to properly "pick" a steamed crab, pulling out the bits of delicious backfin and claw meat. The activity is not to be hurried. The idea is to sit and enjoy, drink iced tea or beer or soda, and perhaps supplement the crabs with an ear or two of sweet corn or a bowl of tomato-based Maryland crab soup.

Do not, however, supplement too much, for eating the crabs is the fun part. Expect to sit for a few hours telling stories and talking while you eat. Having a crab feast is more like a party than just a meal.

You'll likely have the table, whether inside or out, covered with thick brown paper or old newspapers. This makes it easy to pick up all the leftover shells and discard the resulting mess. Restaurants often use several layers of paper, peeling away the dirty layers as the eating continues.

Again, this may seem bizarre to outsiders, but it's tradition, it's pleasurable, it's delicious, and it's unique to the Chesapeake and Delaware Bay region.

Picking techniques vary slightly, but the basics involve removing the apron and pulling off the outer shell. You discard the devil and pull off the claws and smaller legs. Many experts set the claws aside to eat last; if you eat them early, your hands will get covered with too much Old Bay.

Break the remaining crab in half and dig into the cartilage-like shell that remains, eating pieces of delectable crabmeat as you pull them out.

Take your time. This is a leisurely pursuit, and even out-of-towners have been known to develop a penchant for steamed crabs. Of course, it helps to have a local teach you the ropes. Once you get the hang of it, it's easy, fun, and delicious.

The lights themselves. **Thomas Point Shoal Light** is a screwpile-style lighthouse built in 1875; it is the third light to exist on the site. (Screwpile lighthouses are built on a foundation of iron legs screwed to the bottom of the bay and protected by piles of stones.) It became a historic landmark in 1975 and has the distinction of being the most photographed lighthouse on the bay.

Sandy Point Shoal Light was built in 1883; the current caisson-style lighthouse is the second on the site. (A caisson lighthouse is built on a cast-iron cylinder, called a caisson, that is sunk into the bottom of the bay.) In June 2006, this light was sold at auction to a private owner for $250,000. Private ownership lends credence to the romantic notions many people have about lighthouses. Unfortunately, this light is falling into disrepair due to neglect.

Baltimore Harbor Light (officially Baltimore Light), built in 1908, was the last lighthouse built on the Chesapeake Bay. It was the tallest caisson-style light in the world at the time, and it's the only light on the bay ever powered by atomic energy (for a year or so as an experiment in the 1960s). This lighthouse is also privately owned and is well maintained. So, private ownership can be good or bad depending upon the owners and the care they take (or not) of their acquisitions.

On the route out of and into Stevensville, the boat passes beneath the two spans of **Chesapeake Bay Bridge** twice, presenting a unique perspective for those who have only driven across it previously.

The first span of the bridge was completed in 1952, the second in 1973. Previously, crossing the bay was an exercise that required taking a steamboat ferry or driving around the top of the bay.

Each span is 4.3 miles long, with a ship clearance of 186 feet vertically and 1,500 feet horizontally.

Some additional lights. **Sharps Island Light** is situated on an island that is now underwater and was once as large as 900 acres. The light was built in 1882 as a replacement for an earlier light and was at one time used to house cattle and sheep. This caisson-style light was named for Peter Sharpe, a Quaker physician.

Sharps Island Light is easily recognizable because it's tilted 15 degrees, having been knocked askew by an ice floe in 1977. It sits 3 miles south-southwest off the tip of **Tilghman Island** and can also be seen from land. Though not on the current boat tour, this lighthouse is close by, so it can easily be seen from a chartered boat.

To see it by car, leave from St. Michaels and drive on MD 33 West (which becomes Tilghman Island Road) for about 12 miles. Cross the drawbridge onto Tilghman Island and follow Tilghman Island Road south as far as you can go to Black Walnut Point. Along the way you'll see the lighthouse offshore to your right. If you're hungry, you can stop along the way at **Tilghman Island Country Store**, which makes excellent sandwiches to go.

Another interesting light that's nearby but not on the current tour is **Bloody Point Bar Light** located below the tip of Kent Island. The name's exact origin is unknown, but stories abound. In one version, white settlers allegedly invited a local Indian tribe, probably the Matapeakes, into their settlement. Once the Indians got there, the settlers brutally massacred them.

According to another tale, some local pirates were hanged at the tip of Kent Island, thus lending "bloody" to the name.

The third story is that a skipjack captain swept his crew overboard with the ship's boom at the end of dredging season rather than paying them for their labor.

Three great stories—take your pick as to which one you choose to believe.

Bloody Point is also a caisson design and is considered a sister light to the one on Sharps Island. Bloody Point is certainly a contender for generating the most stories, or at least the most colorful stories, of all the lights.

If you like boats and the water, seeing the lighthouses on a boat tour is great fun. If you're a real aficionado, Chesapeake Lighthouses occasionally offers longer, all-day trips and even some overnight two-day excursions that feature more lights. Or you can book the boat for a private charter that includes your choice of different lighthouses.

After your boat tour, head to one of the excellent restaurants in Easton or St. Michaels. It's large and a bit touristy, but the **Crab Claw** in St. Michaels is a great place to have steamed blue crabs and talk about the lighthouses, sports, or anything else that suits you. Or close to the Bay Bridge Marina, options for partaking of the iconic steamed crabs include **Harris Crabhouse & Seafood Restaurant.** The next morning, enjoy breakfast, check out and begin viewing more lighthouses from the road.

Lighthouses on Land

While you're in St. Michaels, stop to see the **Hooper Strait Lighthouse**, a screwpile light from 1879 that you can climb and tour. In 1900, there were more than 40 screwpile lights in the bay, but only a few remain today. This lighthouse was moved from its original site and relocated to the grounds of the **Chesapeake Bay Maritime Museum** on the Miles River. You'll see the entrance on the left-hand side as you drive out of St. Michaels on MD 33 East.

After you stop at the museum, continue on MD 33 East and turn right onto Easton Parkway. From there, take the ramp onto US 50 East. Cross the Choptank River Bridge (officially the Senator Frederick C. Malkus, Jr. Bridge) into **Cambridge** to see the **Choptank River Replica Lighthouse**. The replica light is in the Cambridge marina beside the beautiful Choptank River, in full view of the US 50 bridge. The marina is filled with pleasure boats and workboats. Visitors can climb the staircase to the light to admire the view; there are also interesting exhibits inside.

To get there, after the Malkus Bridge turn right onto Maryland Avenue, cross the Cambridge Creek Bridge, make a right on Academy Street, and turn right again onto High Street.

For purists, reconstructed and replica lighthouses are not the same as the originals. For those who just like lighthouses and enjoy being in a beautiful spot by the water, this is a worthwhile stop.

The original Choptank River Lighthouse was the only lighthouse on the river that guided ships from Baltimore to Cambridge, Oxford, and Denton. From the late 1880s to World War I, the river was traveled by steamboats that came from Baltimore and stopped at Long Wharf in Cambridge to pick up produce, seafood, and passengers. The trip back to Baltimore took place overnight and was a unique excursion for those on board.

Located about 7 miles up the Choptank River from the mouth of the Chesapeake Bay, the original lighthouse was situated around hidden shoals near Benoni Point. In 1918, an ice storm destroyed the first Choptank River Light, which had operated since 1871. A second light was installed in 1921 and remained in use until it was removed in 1964 as part of a modernization plan. The current replica was built from official drawings of the second screwpile light.

The original lighthouse was accessible only by boat, as it was 2 miles from land. The replica has exterior steps, but in the original, the lighthouse keeper had to use a winch to hoist his boat to the deck level.

In James Michener's novel *Chesapeake,* the Patamoke Light is modeled on the Choptank River Light.

Next on the agenda is **Hooper Island**. From Cambridge, get back on US 50 East and fill up your gas tank before you go any farther. The place you're going next is remote, and there won't be an opportunity to get gasoline.

On US 50, you'll soon see a Walmart on your right. At the light just past the Walmart, turn right onto MD 16 West (Church Creek Road). (If you turn left, you'll be on Heron Boulevard, which is the entrance to the **Hyatt Regency Chesapeake Bay Golf Resort, Spa & Marina.**)

Follow MD 16 West until you turn left onto MD 335 South (Hoopers Island Road). The road twists and turns a bit, but it will lead you to Hooper Island. (Note that in some places it's "Hooper," in others it's "Hooper's" or "Hoopers." Just go with the flow.)

The drive to Hooper Island will take about an hour or a little less through part of **Blackwater National Wildlife Refuge.** This is an isolated route with extensive marshes, a few farms, and water always nearby. This is most definitely lowland, and if a storm is bad enough, it will flood. Absent a storm, the refuge is a wonderful place to drive, hike, or bike along the **Blackwater River** to observe birds and evocative scenery.

On the way to Hooper Island, you'll also pass the **Harriet Tubman**

Underground Railroad State Park and Visitor Center. The center's museum honors Tubman's legacy in leading and liberating slaves from the region to freedom at her own peril. In a clever architectural design, the visitor center is aligned from north to south. Visitors enter in the southern portion of the building and make their way north like Tubman did. There's a subtle hint of optimism as one progresses through the exhibits, with more light and higher ceilings as you go further north in the building.

South of Blackwater, you'll reach Hooper Island. By the way, locals pronounce the name of their island *huh-per* (sounds like *hooker*, but with a *p* instead of a *k*). If you say *who-per*, someone is bound to correct you or give a good-natured smile and shake their head.

Hooper Island was once larger and more vibrant, but it's still an active watermen's community. Like Smith and Tangier Islands, the locals speak a form of old Elizabethan English that can be hard for visitors to understand; they tend to talk fast too, making them even harder to follow. By concentrating and asking residents to repeat themselves, you can usually get the gist.

The name of the island is not the only word that has special pronunciation. Oyster fritters are *oster flitters,* and this part of the world is the Eastern *Sure.* The island, once known as Baron Island, is referred to locally as *Barnt* Island.

There are actually three islands that make up Hooper Island—the upper, middle, and lower islands. From Blackwater National Wildlife Refuge, there's a bridge at Tylers Cove over Fishing Creek that leads onto the upper island. You'll notice an old bank building that is now someone's house on the right-hand side of the road.

The amazing setting is awe-inspiring, with the Chesapeake Bay on one side and **Back Creek**, a tributary of the **Honga River**, on the other side of the small fishing village appropriately called **Fishing Creek**. You'll be overwhelmed, in a good way, by the closeness of the Chesapeake Bay on one side of the island and Back Creek on the other. Maybe only 100 yards or so of land separates them.

If you have kids with you, or if you just have a whimsical nature, keep an eye out for unusual and entertaining mailbox decor—there are several clever and appealing boxes. Not all residents have an unusual mailbox, but enough do to make for an interesting search.

There are also egrets, herons, and Canada geese all around. You'll want to stop at **Old Salty's Restaurant** first thing for a wonderful lunch. Order anything with crab and you won't be disappointed. It's fresh, the dishes are superb, and it's open year-round.

Instead of the rickety wooden structure you're likely to expect out in the middle of seemingly nowhere and with a name like Old Salty's, the building is well kept. It was built as a schoolhouse in the 1920s. At one point it had only 11 grades, with the 12th grade mandated around 1941.

If you're lucky enough to get a seat by the window, your view will include a duck blind right out in the Chesapeake. The locals usually sit at the bar, so diners in the restaurant are most likely from somewhere else. The crabcakes are so wonderful that many are willing to drive a long distance to eat here on a semi-regular basis.

There's a gift shop inside the restaurant building too. Though small, it has a good selection of local books and crafts for sale.

After lunch, turn right out of the parking area and continue farther down the island to see the variety of boats, including those used for fishing, crabbing, and oystering, as well as many others that are used mainly for recreation. There are a few churches too, as well as a house designed to look like a lighthouse, with the bay just feet away.

If you continue driving, you'll come to another bridge that seemingly rises out of the water. As you cross the dramatic **Narrows Ferry Bridge**, you're at the intersection of the bay and the Honga River. To your right, in the distance, is **Hooper Island Light**, 3 miles offshore in the bay. Drive a bit farther and you'll see some rocky breakwaters with birds sitting on top.

Some visitors are disappointed the lighthouse is so far in the distance. But a visit to Hooper Island, especially if you travel across the second bridge and farther south, is an amazing experience in itself. It's almost as close as you can get to having the bay to yourself without actually being out on the water.

Hooper Island Light began operating in 1902. It stands 63 feet above the water and sits in 18 feet of water. It's a pneumatic, cast-iron caisson-style light that still operates with a solar-powered optic. You can see it from the island, faintly, with the naked eye. A telephoto lens on a camera or binoculars will help, but this light is best seen from on board a charter boat.

Once you cross this second bridge, you're on the middle island, also known as **Hoopersville**. Toward the end of Hoopersville, you'll pass Steam Boat Wharf Road on your left.

When you feel like you're experiencing déjà vu because you see Steam Boat Wharf Road on your left again, take that left and follow the road around. It does a U-turn and will bring you back to the main road, which is Hoopersville Road. Turn right and head back out of this gorgeous, dramatic spot of land with amazing views. Or turn left and travel about a mile to reach **Riverside Lodge**. Some men gather at the lodge to hunt deer and waterfowl from mid-November through the end of January. With five rooms and a bungalow for rent, the men can stay there to hunt and drink beer.

The rest of the year, the lodge is available to others as a base for boating and fishing. "If it's on a boat, we can do it," says one of the owners. At the lodge, a charter boat will take you across the bay to **Solomons Island** or down the bay to **Smith Island** for lunch. Or you can go fishing, crabbing, and jet skiing. The lodge is a bit rugged. If you need luxury, you can stay at the Hyatt in Cambridge and drive down, engaging Riverside Lodge to facilitate your water activities.

From Hoopersville, you can't drive any farther. The third island of Hooper Island is uninhabited, accessible only by boat or ATV. Occasionally hunters go there to shoot ducks, geese, and a few deer; it is strictly private property.

Some say Hooper Island is reminiscent of Tilghman Island, the watermen's community a bit farther north. While that is a reasonable comparison, Hooper Island is more akin to the utterly isolated Smith Island, which is south of Hooper Island in the middle of the Chesapeake Bay.

On Hooper Island, anyone who lives north of the bridge at Tylers Cove leading onto the upper island is considered a foreigner. Then there's the out-of-time Elizabethan-like speech, which is similar to the dialect spoken on Smith Island. And the totally insular nature of the two places is comparable. Of course, you can drive or cycle on and off Hooper Island, whereas the only access to Smith Island is by boat.

As you might guess, there was once a steamboat wharf on Hooper Island, and commercial activity was much more intense than it is today. Locally grown tomatoes and locally caught blue crabs—along with everything else produced on the Eastern Shore—were shipped via steamer to Baltimore. When the steamers returned, they brought goods back for the dozen or so grocery stores on the island at the time.

There are still a handful of crab picking and processing plants on Hooper Island. Temporary workers are brought in from April through October; they go home when the crabs stop coming in. That leaves just the watermen here year-round, and they often do it all—oystering, crabbing, and fishing. If it swims or exists in the bay, they'll catch it across all seasons.

Hooper Island, with Old Salty's, its working waterfront, and all its gorgeous views, makes for an enjoyable excursion. Viewing the lighthouse, although it's far out in the bay, is just extra. If you want to get a close-up view of the light by boat, Riverside Lodge can arrange it for you.

Bring bikes if you want to pedal along this authentic bit of shoreline. Just be aware that this is a narrow stretch of land where the tide comes up and goes back, as it has for centuries.

With the sea level rising and erosion taking place daily, the remaining land is even more precious. Perched on the edge of water that's constantly lapping against its shore, the island exists in a delicate balance between nature and the friendly folks who make this home.

To return to the Chesapeake Bay Bridge, get on MD 335 North and follow it back to MD 16 East. At the intersection with US 50, turn left to go west and back toward the bridge.

If you want to extend your trip an extra night, there is a lovely B&B in Cambridge—**Cambridge House Bed & Breakfast**. There's also the excellent Hyatt. There are several good spots for dinner, too, including **Bistro Poplar**, **Jimmie & Sook's**, and **Canvasback**.

IN THE AREA

Annapolis

Attractions and Recreation

ANNAPOLIS MARITIME MUSEUM, (excursions to Thomas Point Shoal Light from the Western Shore). Call 415-362-7255. Website: amaritime.org/museum/thomas-point-lighthouse.

Cambridge

Accommodations

CAMBRIDGE HOUSE BED & BREAKFAST. Call 410-221-7700. Website: www.cambridgehousebandb.com.

HYATT REGENCY CHESAPEAKE BAY GOLF RESORT, SPA & MARINA. Call 410-901-1234. Website: hyatt.com/en-US/hotel/maryland/hyatt-regency -chesapeake-bay-golf-resort-spa-and-marina/chesa.

Attractions and Recreation

BLACKWATER NATIONAL WILDLIFE REFUGE VISITOR CENTER. Call 410-228-2677. Website: fws.gov/refuge/Blackwater.

CHOPTANK RIVER REPLICA LIGHTHOUSE. Call 410-463-2653. Website: choptankriverlighthouse.org.

HARRIET TUBMAN UNDERGROUND RAILROAD STATE PARK AND VISITOR CENTER. Call 410-221-2290. Website: dnr.maryland.gov/public lands/Pages/eastern/tubman.aspx.

Dining/Drinks

BISTRO POPLAR. Call 410-228-4884. Website: www.bistropoplar.com.

CANVASBACK RESTAURANT & IRISH PUB. Call 410-221-7888.

JIMMIE & SOOK'S RAW BAR AND GRILL. Call 410-228-0008. Website: jimmieandsooks.com.

Easton

Accommodations

TIDEWATER INN. Call 410-822-1300 or 1-800-237-8775 (reservations). Website: www.tidewaterinn.com.

Dining/Drinks

OUT OF THE FIRE. Call 410-770-4777. Website: www.outofthefire.com.

Grasonville

Dining/Drinks

HARRIS CRABHOUSE & SEAFOOD RESTAURANT. Call 410-827-9500. Website: harriscrabhouse.com.

Hooper Island

Attractions and Recreation

HOOPER ISLAND LIGHT.

RIVERSIDE LODGE. Call 410-658-4868. Website: riversidelodgemd.com.

Dining/Drinks

OLD SALTY'S RESTAURANT. Call 410-397-3752. Website: oldsaltys.com.

Solomons Island

Attractions and Recreation

CALVERT MARINE MUSEUM, (with relocated Drum Point Light-house; Cove Point Lighthouse also nearby; excursions to lighthouses from the Western Shore). Call 410-326-2042 (ext. 41). Website: www .calvertmarinemuseum.com/239/Lighthouse-Cruises.

WATERMEN HERITAGE TOURS. Website: www.watermenheritagetours .org.

St. Michaels

Accommodations

INN AT PERRY CABIN. Call 410-745-2200 or 1-888-805-8885. Website: innatperrycabin.com.

Attractions and Recreation

CHESAPEAKE BAY MARITIME MUSEUM, (with relocated Hooper Strait Lighthouse). Call 410-745-2916. Website: www.cbmm.org.

Dining/Drinks

AVA'S PIZZERIA & WINE BAR. Call 410-745-3081. Website: www.avas pizzeria.com.

THE CRAB CLAW RESTAURANT. Call 410-745-2900. Website: thecrabclaw .com.

Stevensville

Attractions and Recreation

CHESAPEAKE LIGHTHOUSES. Call 413-835-1630. Website: www .chesapeakelights.com.

Dining/Drinks

HEMINGWAY'S RESTAURANT. Call 410-604-0999. Website: hemingways baybridge.com.

LOVE POINT DELI. Call 410-604-2447. Website: www.lovepointdeli.com.

Tilghman Island

Attractions and Recreation

SHARPS ISLAND LIGHT.

Dining/Drinks

TILGHMAN ISLAND COUNTRY STORE. Call 410-886-2777. Website: tilghmanisland.com/bars-restaurants/tilghman-island-country-store.

2

VISITING FORMER STEAMBOAT LANDINGS

ESTIMATED LENGTH: 240 miles round-trip

ESTIMATED TIME: 2–3 days

GETTING THERE: From Annapolis, take US 50 East. Cross the Chesapeake Bay Bridge to the Eastern Shore and continue on US 50. Stay to the right when US 50 becomes Ocean Gateway and splits with US 301 North. Turn left onto MD 404 East until you reach Denton, where you'll turn right onto River Road and left onto River Landing Road.

    Follow the winding road, though it may seem as if you're in the wrong place. Keep going past the unassuming yacht club on the left and some houses on the right. Continue until you reach the orange wharf building on the left beside the **Choptank River**. If school's out, there may be some local boys fishing from the dock.

HIGHLIGHTS: Replica steamboat wharf and museum in Denton; old Tolchester Beach bandstand at the Chesapeake Bay Maritime Museum in St. Michaels; Claiborne steamboat landing site north of Tilghman Island; exhibit at Choptank River Replica Lighthouse; Chesapeake Beach on the Western Shore.

The introduction of the steamboat to the Chesapeake Bay and the region's rivers in the early 1800s was a major advancement in travel. Steamboats were able to transport passengers and freight relatively quickly and efficiently.

The old ways were changing, and extreme isolation was becoming a thing of the past. Steamers, as many called them, could move people and products without being as dependent on the vagaries of the weather as they were in the past with sailing vessels.

HERON ON THE CHOPTANK RIVER

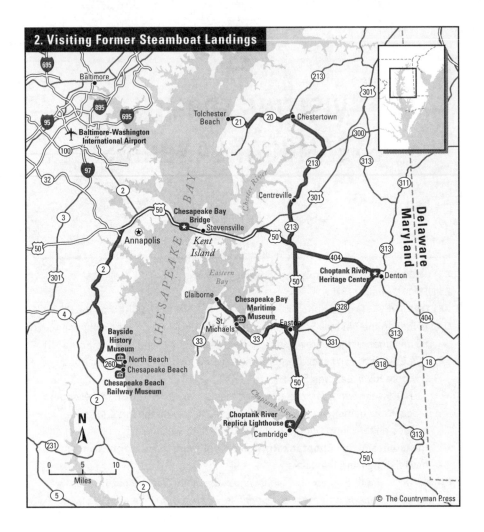

Steam engines began to appear in vessels on the Chesapeake around 1813. By 1817, steamboats were regularly scheduled. With schedules, plans could be made. This resulted in changes to commerce as well as to social and cultural entertainment.

First, with regard to commerce, Maryland's Eastern Shore was able to thrive due to the new ability to get produce, seafood, and other goods to Baltimore quickly while still fresh. This proved an economic boon to areas with these resources and steamboat landings or even the ability to create a landing.

Second, the waterways provided an exciting new playground for residents of stifling-hot cities, especially Baltimore and, to a lesser extent, Washington, DC. After all, there was no air-conditioning, and the cities were crowded.

FORMER STEAMBOAT LANDING AT TOLCHESTER BEACH

Resorts evolved now that the steamboats could transport city dwellers to a beach, and it was even better if the beach had amusements.

The first stop on this itinerary is the **Choptank River Heritage Center**. The Choptank is the longest river on the Eastern Shore. **Denton** became a commercial trading center, for the area was strictly agricultural and farmers needed to ship their wares to Baltimore and other urban destinations. Having the river was a major economic advantage.

Back in the day, steamboat service was vitally important for transporting the agricultural products grown in abundance up and down the river. The original wharf in West Denton, which is where the heritage center is located, was a major hub, with warehouses, canneries, wharves, and more. In 1882, the Maryland Steamboat Company bought one of the wharves, which is why that name is on the heritage center replica.

Canneries were not unique to Denton, of course. There were also canneries and seafood packinghouses in Cambridge, Tilghman Island, Secretary, Oxford, Sherwood, and elsewhere along the Choptank. First steamboats, then railroads, then trucks brought the products to market. The heyday of the canning era was from the 1880s to the 1940s. Many C rations for the US military during World War II came from a cannery on the Eastern Shore.

You can stand on the pier in West Denton and look out at the river, which is quiet and peaceful, unlike the busy spot it was from the 1880s until the

CAROUSEL ANIMAL FROM CHESAPEAKE BEACH'S PAST

steamboat landing was abandoned in 1912. Blue herons are plentiful, and the spot is utterly charming.

Inside the replica turn-of-the-century steamboat warehouse is a small museum of sorts with memorabilia and exhibits reminiscent of the steamboat era. The waiting area is where passengers and goods would have waited for a steamboat to arrive, probably to take them to Baltimore.

There's also a separate replica of the structure similar to the one where livestock was kept for transport.

There were landings and wharves up and down the Choptank. The one in Denton was a major one and is marked now, but others, long ago abandoned, are less acknowledged.

Restaurants in Denton are rather limited, but one good option is **Market Street Public House**. If the obscurity of Denton appeals to you, the only place to stay over is the **Best Western Denton Inn**.

The heritage center will help you understand a little about the business end of the steamboat era. Equally important was the recreational aspect. In beach towns along the Eastern Shore, steamboat landings caused scores of travelers from Baltimore and other places to cross the Chesapeake Bay to have fun on the beach.

Tolchester Beach is an excellent example of one such beach town. During the steamboat era, apart from the beach, Tolchester boasted a bandstand, amusement park, and other entertainment.

You can drive to Tolchester Beach, which is almost directly across the bay from Baltimore. From Denton, take MD 404 West to MD 213 North to MD 20 West to MD 21 West. Unfortunately, there's nothing much there now except a road that leads to the bay, a bunch of rocks, and a tiny beach.

A better alternative is to drive from Denton to **St. Michaels** by taking MD 328 South to MD 33 West. In St. Michaels, stop at the **Chesapeake Bay Maritime Museum**, which has an impressive campus-like complex.

While there, look at the old Tolchester bandstand, which was relocated from Tolchester Beach to its current spot in front of the Hooper Strait Lighthouse. The lighthouse was also relocated from its original location to these museum grounds beside the Miles River.

MARINA AT CHESAPEAKE BEACH, WHERE THERE WAS ONCE A STEAMBOAT LANDING

The bandstand will give you a sense of the serious nature of big-time entertainment at the former bay resorts.

After spending time at the museum, get back on MD 33 West. Follow it until the road splits—left to Tilghman Island, right to **Claiborne**. Take the right-hand fork onto Claiborne Road and drive about 1.5 miles to Claiborne Landing Road; turn left and continue to the dock.

Again, there's no longer much left in Claiborne. It's pretty, but like most former steamboat landings, Claiborne is quiet and serene—unlike at the apex of the steamboat ferry era, when visitors from Baltimore and the Western Shore took the ferry (or the "steamer") to the village.

Back then, travelers stayed nearby in lodgings provided by farmers during the summer tourist season, or they took the train to Ocean City, with its amenities and the Atlantic Ocean. That train was part of the Baltimore, Chesapeake & Atlantic Railway, with stops in Claiborne, St. Michaels, Easton, and across the Choptank River in Bethlehem, Preston, Hurlock, Vienna, Mardela Springs, Salisbury, and Ocean City.

Of course, the steamboat era was prior to the construction of the

Chesapeake Bay Bridge—the 4.3-mile expanse that connects the Annapolis area to Kent Island by car. Back then, urban dwellers desirous of beach vacations for themselves and their kids headed around the Chesapeake Bay via steamboat.

The result of this steamboat travel was a group of resort-like enclaves like Tolchester Beach that boasted amusement parks, beaches, music, dance halls, food, hotels, and souvenir shops.

From 1885 to 1920, the steamboat *Joppa,* for instance, transported passengers, livestock, and goods to and from the port of Baltimore. Other steamboats included the *Enoch Pratt, Avalon, Cambridge,* and *Ida.* Their stops included Cambridge, which is where you'll head next.

From Claiborne, take MD 33 East past St. Michaels and toward Easton. If you're hungry along the way, **Ava's Pizzeria & Wine Bar** is excellent, and it's right in downtown St. Michaels. From MD 33 East, turn right on Easton Parkway, then take the ramp to US 50 East. Take US 50 across the Choptank River Bridge into Cambridge. Plan to stay at the **Hyatt Regency Chesapeake Bay Golf Resort, Spa & Marina**; it's a lovely property—a modern version of the bay resorts from the past.

You can dine at the Hyatt or go into Cambridge proper for a good meal at **Bistro Poplar**. While in Cambridge, stop by the **Choptank River Replica Lighthouse** on Long Wharf. There's a large marina, free parking, and a lovely view of the bridge and river from the deck of the lighthouse.

Many families boarded steamboats in Baltimore and enjoyed the overnight excursion to Cambridge. The trip offered sea breezes, the sight of lighthouses on the bay, and fancy dining rooms on board, catering to passengers.

Spend a night or two at the Hyatt and enjoy. Just leave time at the end of your trip to visit a former steamboat resort back on the Western Shore.

After you check out of the Hyatt, take US 50 West back across the Chesapeake Bay Bridge. Once across, take MD 2 South to MD 260 East to Chesapeake Beach.

On the Maryland Western Shore, **Chesapeake Beach** and **Baltimore** were two places where steamboats regularly landed. There was train transportation too, but steamboats connected Baltimore and Chesapeake Beach to each other and to the more isolated Eastern Shore.

Baltimore was important for commerce as well as leisure transport; Baltimore was, and still is, *the* major port on the bay. The bayside resort of Chesapeake Beach, built in 1899 south of Annapolis, was focused on pleasure. Its owner, Otto Mears, hoped to have this new town of his rival Atlantic City, New Jersey, and Coney Island, New York. Mears failed to accomplish this goal, but he did manage to create an amusement park, hotel, beach, and mile-long pier and boardwalk with entertainment. He even built a railroad line to Washington, DC.

Visitors from Baltimore came by steamboat. Visitors from Washington rode the train and arrived at the tiny depot, which is still there. The train depot is now the **Chesapeake Beach Railway Museum**, and it has great memorabilia from the steamboat era.

One of the main attractions in Chesapeake Beach was a roller coaster. Great for thrill seekers, it operated from about 1916 to 1926. Over the years, there was often a carousel, or a merry-go-round, too. The boardwalk was lined with restaurants, souvenir shops, amusements, and games of chance.

Absent air-conditioning, thousands of visitors would pour in from the sweltering cities to enjoy the cool breezes off the bay.

Eventually, during the Great Depression of the 1930s, the railroad line built by Mears went out of business, and the steamboat era ended. When all this occurred, the resort at Chesapeake Beach went bust.

In recent years, there's been a revival of sorts in Chesapeake Beach. Today there's a lovely hotel, the **Rod 'N' Reel Resort**, as well as a marina and restaurants. The twin beach of **North Beach**, next door, has its own shops and restaurants, like the superb **Westlawn Inn**, as well as the **Bayside History Museum**, with a collection of colorful relics from the steamboat era.

And though it's on the Western Shore, Chesapeake Beach is reminiscent of the steamboat era that bound the two halves of Maryland together in a new way. Transportation will do that.

From Chesapeake Beach, take MD 260 North to MD 4 West to reach the Beltway around Washington, DC. To access Baltimore from Chesapeake Beach, take MD 260 North to MD 2 North back to US 50 West and I-97.

There were many other steamboat wharves and landings on and around the Chesapeake Bay besides those in this itinerary. Some were regular stops, and others were "sometimes" stops, where if someone wanted a ride, he or she would fly a flag or stand and wave—kind of like a bus stop today. Either way, the excitement surrounding a large steamboat arriving with people and goods must have been quite a sight.

IN THE AREA

Cambridge

Accommodations

HYATT REGENCY CHESAPEAKE BAY GOLF RESORT, SPA & MARINA. Call 410-901-1234. Website: www.hyatt.com/en-US/hotel/maryland/hyatt-regency-chesapeake-bay-golf-resort-spa-and-marina/chesa.

Attractions and Recreation

CHOPTANK RIVER REPLICA LIGHTHOUSE. Call 410-463-2653. Website: www.choptankriverlighthouse.org.

Dining/Drinks

BISTRO POPLAR. Call: 410-228-4884. Website: www.bistropoplar.com.

Chesapeake Beach

Accommodations

ROD 'N' REEL RESORT. Call 410-257-5596 or 1-866-312-5596. Website: www.chesapeakebeachresortspa.com.

Attractions and Recreation

BAYSIDE HISTORY MUSEUM, North Beach. Call 410-610-5970. Website: www.baysidehistorymuseum.org.

CHESAPEAKE BEACH RAILWAY MUSEUM. Call 410-257-3892. Website: chesapeakebeachrailwaymuseum.com.

Dining/Drinks

THE WESTLAWN INN, North Beach. Call 410-257-0001. Website: www.westlawninn.com.

Denton

Accommodations

BEST WESTERN DENTON INN. Call 410-479-8400. Website: www.bestwestern.com/en_US/book/hotels-in-denton/best-western-denton-inn/propertyCode.21046.html.

Attractions and Recreation

CHOPTANK RIVER HERITAGE CENTER. Call 410-479-0655. Website: www.visitcaroline.org/listings/choptank-river-heritage-center.

Dining/Drinks

MARKET STREET PUBLIC HOUSE. Call 410-479-4720. Website: market street.pub.

St. Michaels

Attractions and Recreation

CHESAPEAKE BAY MARITIME MUSEUM, with Tolchester bandstand. Call 410-745-2916. Website: www.cbmm.org.

Dining/Drinks

AVA'S PIZZERIA & WINE BAR. Call 410-745-3081. Website: www.avas pizzeria.com.

3

TRAVELING THE UPPER CHESAPEAKE BAY

ESTIMATED LENGTH: 190 miles round-trip

ESTIMATED TIME: 1 day, though it can be extended to 2–3 days

GETTING THERE: Take I-95 North from Baltimore, cross the Susquehanna River, and pay the toll. Take exit 100 (on I-95 South from Philadelphia, take exit 100A) to MD 272 South and continue to the town of North East.

HIGHLIGHTS: Antiques shopping, Washington College in Chestertown, Rock Hall beach and town, public square in Centreville, Stevensville historic buildings, dinner at Rustico, sunset from Matapeake Fishing Pier.

We're going to start out in North East and travel on to Chesapeake City at the upper reaches of the Chesapeake Bay. Next we'll head down the Eastern Shore to Stevensville and back around to the Chesapeake Bay Bridge.

This trip is for those who enjoy unusually small towns, places where everyone knows everyone else and knows their business. For people from big cities, there is charm in visiting these towns. For those from rural areas or small towns themselves, they will no doubt feel immediately at home.

The trip is ideal for a one-day car excursion beginning on I-95 from Baltimore, Wilmington, Philadelphia, or Washington, DC.

Often when people think of the Maryland Eastern Shore, they automatically smell the salt water in their minds and think of Ocean City. If they are more familiar with the Eastern Shore, they may think of boating on the Miles River outside St. Michaels or on the Chesapeake Bay itself off Tilghman Island.

While those pursuits are wonderful, there's an entire section of the Maryland Eastern Shore north of the Chesapeake Bay Bridge that's quiet, beautiful, and relaxing.

MATAPEAKE FISHING PIER AT SUNSET, WITH A VIEW OF THE CHESAPEAKE BAY BRIDGE

For this trip, we'll start in the northern part and head south. You can reverse the trip if you like; however, doing it this way on a Saturday allows you to go against the heavy traffic heading to the ocean for the weekend. Thus, the drive is more relaxing.

Besides just touring around, you can always go antiquing, which is popular all over the area. Starting with North East and Chesapeake City on the upper shore and encompassing the little towns along the way, you never

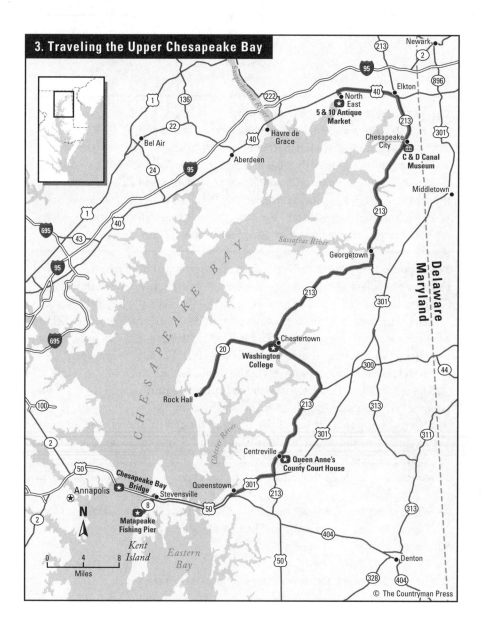

3. Traveling the Upper Chesapeake Bay

© The Countryman Press

know where or when you'll find a little treasure to delight you for days, weeks, or years.

Concentrations of antiques stores are located in North East, Chesapeake City, Chestertown, and Rock Hall. You're likely to find lots of furniture, old books, china, glassware, toys, and jewelry. This is certainly a form of treasure hunting, of looking to find a gem in the midst of items lost, discarded, or sold by others.

In **North East**, there are several interesting shops, chief among them the **5&10 Antique Market**. You can find all kinds of antiques and just plain "old" things here—plenty to occupy some time even if you're just looking and decide not to buy. If it's not too early in the day for lunch, **Woody's Crab House** is a great place to grab something to eat, especially if you're a seafood lover.

If it's too early to have lunch, the next town on the agenda, **Chesapeake City**, has several good restaurants, including **The Bayard House Restaurant**. To get there, take US 40 East (Pulaski Highway). Turn right onto MD 213 South for approximately 6 miles and cross the bridge that's built high

How Old Is Old?

Antiques are traditionally considered anything more than 100 years old; younger items that are still old are considered "vintage." Eventually, everything will become an antique. Collectibles include both antiques and vintage items—basically anything someone wants to collect. And their worth? Whatever someone is willing to pay. Regardless of age or cost, it's best to like what you're buying.

Collecting is an enjoyable hobby, whatever you choose to pursue. The art of the hunt, the discovery of a desirable find inside a dusty box of "junk," the negotiating of a reasonable price—all these increase a collector's pleasure with newly acquired prizes. Value is certainly one aspect of an antique, as is the history that adheres to the item, whether that history is known or unknown. In either case, the antique has a past.

Whether you gravitate toward snuff boxes or costume jewelry, or are attracted by the allure of owning a treasured book or music box, old sheet music, or a child's toy truck, the relationship between an antique and its new owner is unique. You'll find some interesting places to look for whatever you collect in the part of Maryland's Eastern Shore covered in this excursion.

Part of the fascination we have with old things is that many of them are now long gone. Those that remain share a survivor's place of honor. With few left, those that do exist possess a quirky charm, and their often-laughable utility in our age of high technology adds to the appeal.

YARN SHOP IN CHESAPEAKE CITY

over the **Chesapeake & Delaware (C&D) Canal**. The **Chesapeake City Bridge** is especially high so that huge cargo ships can pass underneath it with no worries.

Once off the bridge, turn right and curve around, continuing to go right after the yield sign and back under the bridge. At the stop sign, turn left onto George Street and then right onto Fourth Street. Make a left on Bohemia Avenue and look for a free on-street visitor parking space.

Large container ships travel the 14-mile canal to shave 300 miles off a trip between Baltimore and Philadelphia. Prior to the canal's opening in 1829, ships had to traverse the Delaware River, Delaware Bay, and Atlantic Ocean to get to the Chesapeake Bay. The journey was made much easier once the canal was built.

Chesapeake City is quiet, charming, and a bit contradictory, with busy recreational and commercial traffic on the canal and a slow, easy pace in the tiny village on the south side. Spend some time looking for antiques or just watching the activity on the canal. It's picturesque, and the people are friendly.

Back on the road again, you're basically going to follow MD 213 South down the peninsula until you're level with the Chesapeake Bay Bridge and heading back home. There will, of course, be a few detours, and you can always wing it on your own.

This is a beautiful area with farms interspersed with waterways, no crowds, and pleasant people. What's not to like?

Heading south on MD 213, you'll next come to **Georgetown**, a river port on the **Sassafras River**. During the War of 1812, the British attacked and burned most of the town. There's no sign of conflict anymore, and the town remains resilient.

Feel free to stop along the way if anything strikes your fancy, or just stay in the car and keep moving if you're enjoying the drive. You will pass a few villages not mentioned here, but as long as you're still on MD 213, you're on the right track.

Next up is **Chestertown**, a charming college town on the **Chester River**. Here it is definitely advisable to park and get out of the car, if for no other reason than to enjoy the river views up close.

Chestertown has an extremely walkable Main Street, so stretch your legs and walk around.

For a snack, **Evergrain Bread Company** on High Street specializes in artisanal breads and European-style pastries. And if you're looking for a good cup of coffee, head to **Play It Again Sam** on Cross Street. If you're there on Saturday, you can visit the **Chestertown Farmers' Market** at Fountain Park.

Washington College is a big part of Chestertown. Founded in 1782 with

CHESTER RIVER WATERFRONT IN CHESTERTOWN

the help of George Washington, it's one of the oldest liberal arts colleges in the United States.

Antiques stores are scattered around on High and Cannon Streets. You can look for fun furnishings and accessories.

From Chestertown, take MD 20 West (High Street) to **Rock Hall**, which is on the Chesapeake Bay. In Rock Hall, there's a tiny public beach and a cute, nostalgic downtown.

Rock Hall had a steamboat ferry landing back in the era when steamers were the mode of transportation across the bay. Now there are several marinas in town for pleasure boating, so it's a friendly, relaxed place.

Waterman's Crab House is a good spot for the view or for eating crabs and drinking beer. Another good choice is the **Inn at Osprey Point** for excellent food.

Next go back toward Chestertown on MD 20 East and pick up MD 213 South, stopping in **Centreville**, with its quaint town square, the oldest courthouse in Maryland, and an interesting statue of Queen Anne. (This is the capital of Maryland's Queen Anne's County, so the statue's placement is understandable.) Stop for a few minutes to walk by **Queen Anne's County Court House** and look at the statue.

Once back on MD 213 South, you'll soon reach US 301 South to the Chesapeake Bay Bridge. But before crossing the bridge, first make a stop in **Stevensville** for dinner. To get there, take the last exit before the bridge, which is MD 8 North. Follow it for a short while to Stevensville, where you'll turn right onto Main Street and left onto Love Point Road.

Stevensville is a tiny hamlet near the Bay Bridge. Walk around the few blocks of historic buildings on and around Love Point Road, and make sure to see the train depot. Then go to **Rustico Restaurant & Wine Bar**, right near the old depot, for exquisite Italian food, especially great pasta.

Rustico is cozy, with both indoor and outdoor (in appropriate weather) seating. It's best to have a reservation on a Saturday evening unless you dine really early, like around 5 p.m.

After dinner and before you go back over the Bay Bridge, if it's still light out, drive to the **Matapeake Fishing Pier** to see the gorgeous sunset over the bay. From Stevensville, drive south on MD 8 South 3 or 4 miles, then turn right at the sign for the pier. Drive a short distance to the parking lot. Sunset from the pier is a sight you'll never forget.

This itinerary is designed to be completed in one day, but that can certainly be extended. If you want to stay over along the way, some desirable accommodations can be found in Chestertown at the **Brampton Bed & Breakfast Inn** or **White Swan Tavern**. In Rock Hall, the Inn at Osprey Point is a good option.

IN THE AREA

Centreville

Attractions and Recreation

QUEEN ANNE'S COUNTY COURT HOUSE, with statue of Queen Anne in front.

Chesapeake City

Dining/Drinks

THE BAYARD HOUSE RESTAURANT. Call 410-885-5040. Website: www .bayardhouse.com.

Chestertown

Accommodations

BRAMPTON BED & BREAKFAST INN. Call 410-778-1860. Website: www .bramptoninn.com.

WHITE SWAN TAVERN. Call 410-778-2300. Website: www.whiteswan tavern.com.

Attractions and Recreation

CHESTERTOWN FARMERS' MARKET. Call 410-778-0500 (Town Hall). Website: chestertownfarmersmarket.net.

WASHINGTON COLLEGE. Call 410-778-2800 or 1-800-422-1782. Website: www.washcoll.edu.

Dining/Drinks

EVERGRAIN BREAD COMPANY. Call 410-778-3333.

PLAY IT AGAIN SAM. Call 410-778-2688. Website: playagainsam.com.

Matapeake

Attractions and Recreation

MATAPEAKE FISHING PIER.

North East

Attractions and Recreation

5&10 ANTIQUE MARKET. Call 410-287-8318. Website: www.5and10 antiques.com.

Dining/Drinks

WOODY'S CRAB HOUSE. Call 410-287-3541. Website: www.woodyscrab house.com.

Rock Hall

Accommodations

INN AT OSPREY POINT. Call 410-639-2194. Website: www.ospreypoint .com.

Dining/Drinks

INN AT OSPREY POINT. Call 410-639-2194. Website: www.ospreypoint .com.

WATERMAN'S CRAB HOUSE. Call 410-639-2261. Website: www .watermanscrabhouse.com.

Stevensville

Attractions and Recreation

HISTORIC TRAIN DEPOT.

Dining/Drinks

RUSTICO RESTAURANT & WINE BAR. Call 410-643-9444. Website: www
.rusticoonline.com.

4

ENJOYING TRAINS, PLANES, AND NASCAR

ESTIMATED LENGTH: 250 miles round-trip

ESTIMATED TIME: 2–3 days

GETTING THERE: From the Chesapeake Bay Bridge, follow US 50 East, then make a left onto MD 404 East. In Hillsboro, turn left onto MD 480 (Ridgely Road) and follow it into the town of Ridgely. Turn left onto Central Avenue and cross the railroad tracks to park.

HIGHLIGHTS: Former railroad towns of Ridgely, Easton, and Delmar; Air Mobility Command Museum at Dover Air Force Base; "The Monster Mile" NASCAR track at Dover International Speedway; peach baron mansion in Magnolia; Fifer Orchards.

Many little boys and girls love trains and planes. When they grow up, they often still love them. This trip has something to offer everyone of any age.

The importance of transportation cannot be overestimated. After all, goods and passengers need access. We may enjoy remote, isolated places, but we still need to be able to get there.

The automobile is certainly a wonderful way to explore. But back in an earlier era, train travel was the epitome of convenience and comfort. Travelers took their time getting to where they were going, enjoying the landscape passing by.

Most of us are charmed by trains. To little kids, they are choo-choos. To the rest of us, they are reminiscent of a slower time when people weren't in so much of a hurry, or perhaps they just had no other option to get there any faster.

The Delmarva Peninsula, with all its waterways, came into its own in

PEACHES FOR SALE AT FIFER ORCHARDS

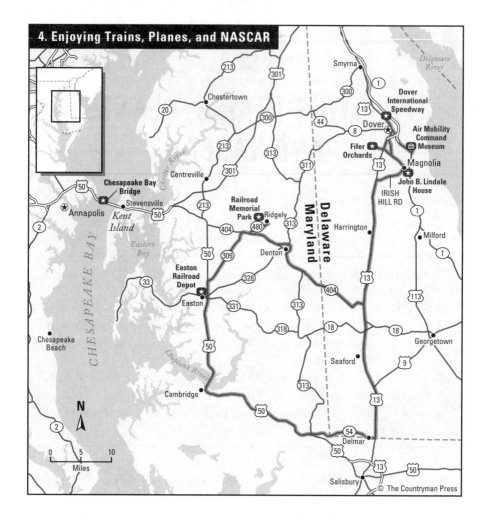

many ways when train tracks crossed the landscape. Even though there are no large train museums here like those in Baltimore or Scranton, Pennsylvania, there are many small train depots and bits of memorabilia that offer a nostalgic glimpse into the importance of the rails.

Either Ridgely or Easton will make a good stop for a nod to the railroads of the past. Or visit both, if trains are truly your passion.

On the Maryland Eastern Shore, **Ridgely** was once a railroad town and is now a quiet little place to take a break from driving. In the downtown area, there's a quaint railroad depot in the middle of **Railroad Memorial Park**. For lunch, try the **Ridgely Pharmacy & Ice Cream Parlor**—certainly a blast from the past that will no doubt have your kids laughing.

There are only about 10 stools at the counter, but the food is pretty good. The menu includes offerings such as a chicken wrap, a salad, or a BLT, plus ice cream, of course. If it's crowded or the weather is good, you can get the food to go and eat outside in the little railroad park across the street.

With its prosperous agricultural business during the railroad era, Ridgely was once considered the Strawberry Capital of the World. That distinction is now gone, but town residents are still proud to hold an **annual strawberry festival** in May.

You can see another quaint **railroad depot** in the town of **Easton**. The Easton depot is being used as an office building now. Having an office in an old train station is an intriguing concept for train lovers.

To get to Easton from Ridgely, take MD 480 West to MD 309 South to US 50 East.

The restored rail station in historic Easton is easy to find. From US 50 East, turn right onto Goldsborough Street. The former depot is on the left as you drive into town.

Because it's an office building now, you cannot go inside, but it's still fun to see from the outside. It's also the beginning point of a rails-to-trails biking and jogging trail along the railroad bed.

In downtown Easton, look for **Hill's Café & Juice Bar**, an old-fashioned soda fountain inside Hill's Drug Store, where you can get a great lunch for a low price, somewhat similar to the experience at the Ridgely Pharmacy. Of course, Easton is a larger town.

At one time, the railroad provided visitors from the Western Shore with transportation from the steamboat landing in Claiborne to Ocean City, passing through Easton on the way. Previously, Easton was very isolated, with most of the townspeople never having been to the Western Shore. Residents felt they had everything they needed on the Eastern Shore—hunting, fishing, and farming. When the railroad arrived, it changed the town, and Easton has since changed even more. Many of the homes are now owned by families whose main residences are in Washington, DC, New York, Pennsylvania, and even Europe.

Though many travelers think Easton is composed only of the stoplights, gasoline stations, and McDonald's they see when driving on US 50, that's merely on the highway, not representative of the town. There are great bed-and-breakfasts, upscale restaurants, and numerous art galleries, so Easton is a good place to take a break when traffic is heavy on US 50, stop for a meal, or stay overnight. It's certainly worth a few hours to see the train depot, have a sandwich at Hill's, and walk around. If you prefer a hotel to a B&B, stay at the **Tidewater Inn**. And you can't go wrong having dinner at **Out of the Fire**.

A visit is likely to entice you to return next time you're going to, or coming from, Ocean City. Of course, more beachgoers stop in Easton on the way home from Ocean City; the lure of salt water and sand is often too tantalizing to delay on the way there.

The town of **Delmar**, which is half in Maryland and half in Delaware along

FORMER PEACH BARON'S MANSION IN MAGNOLIA

the state line, is another former railroad town. Like Ridgely, Delmar was at one time known for its strawberries, but it was called the Strawberry Capital of the United States, not of the world.

Both towns were famous for the abundance of strawberries grown and shipped from their respective areas. One may reasonably wonder how many other railroad towns were given, or gave themselves, similar titles.

From Ridgely, you can reach Delmar by taking MD 480 to MD 404 East. A little while after you cross into Delaware, take US 13 South to MD 54 West.

Alternatively, from Easton you can reach Delmar by taking US 50 East to MD 54 East (Delmar Road). You'll cross the Delaware border after about 3 miles. Continue on DE 54 (Delmar Road) another 6 miles or so.

Once you cross the railroad tracks going east, you're in the town of Delmar (Delmar Road becomes East State Street). After the tracks, immediately turn left onto North Penn Avenue. You'll see a tiny **park** on your left with an old railroad car, a refurbished crossing guard shack, and an antiquated highball symbol—an early railroad device used for signaling to the engineer that all was clear on the tracks.

The railroad industry in Delaware came about primarily to transport produce to Philadelphia and other places. The tracks ran north and south, coinciding with the location of peach orchards throughout the state. Delaware was known as the Peach State before Georgia. Unfortunately, blight hit the Delaware peach farms around 1908, decimating the industry.

After the blight, small towns such as Bridgeville, Camden-Wyoming, Woodside, and Middletown, as well as the state capital of Dover, were left with less busy railroads and big "peach mansions" near the tracks. These mansions were built by the "peach barons"—peach growers who made their fortunes from the sale of the popular fruit during the crop's heyday.

One remarkable peach mansion is in the town of **Magnolia**, which has a sign proclaiming it THE CENTER OF THE UNIVERSE.

The Magnolia peach mansion was built for John Lindale in 1905 and is also known as the John B. Lindale House; it's an interesting example of Victorian architecture. Lindale was one of the peach barons who owned thousands of acres of land in middle and lower Delaware. Lindale's acreage was spread out over 16 farms.

To reach the Lindale peach mansion when traveling from Delmar, continue driving through Delmar on DE 54 East. Turn left onto US 13 North (DuPont Highway), right onto Irish Hill Road, and right again onto South Main Street. The Lindale House is about an eighth of a mile on the left at 24 South Main Street.

If seeing the mansion gets you in the mood for eating peaches, you can drive to **Fifer Orchards** (in the town of Camden-Wyoming) by going northwest on South Main Street, which will become South State Street. Turn left onto Rising Sun Road, followed by another left on West Lebanon Road (DE 10 West) and another on Camden-Wyoming Avenue. Turn right onto South Railroad Avenue (DE 15). Take the first left, Grant Street, which becomes Allabands Mill Road.

Fifer Orchards is on the right. If it's peach season, you're in luck. Even if it's not, Fifer is open April through December selling other produce in season (apples, blueberries, and much more), freshly brewed coffee, and baked goods.

The next stop on the itinerary is Dover. From Magnolia, take South State Street to US 13 North (DuPont Highway). From Fifer Orchards, turn left onto Allabands Mill Road, then right onto North Railroad Avenue, left onto Camden-Wyoming Avenue, and left onto US 13 (DuPont Highway). **Dover International Speedway** and **Dover Downs Hotel & Casino** will be on your right.

If you want to see more Victorian architecture, there's a historic district in downtown Dover that's interesting. You'll also want to check into Dover Downs Hotel & Casino, where you can get a good night's sleep in a lovely hotel and also enjoy slots and table games, numerous restaurant options including the popular **Michele's**, and entertainment. There are restaurants around the city too, including **Cool Springs Fish Bar & Restaurant**.

If you're in the Dover area on a Thursday, there's a fascinating tour of the Dover International Speedway, located adjacent to Dover Downs Hotel & Casino. Home to two NASCAR races—one in May or June and one

ICONIC STATUE OUTSIDE NASCAR'S "MONSTER MILE" IN DOVER

sometime in August to October—the track is well known to racing fans as "The Monster Mile." Thursday is the only day the tour is offered, however, so figure that into your plans. You may need to start your weekend early to fit it in.

For those who like to visit sports stadiums and arenas, this is a must-see. Even if you're not a NASCAR aficionado, the tour is interesting. As a sports venue that can accommodate more than 110,000 spectators, the speedway is a fascinating place to visit, just to give you a sense of the atmosphere. With this unique perspective, you'll never again watch a race on television without remembering how it felt to be there.

The tour takes you out onto Monster Bridge; unique to this sport, Monster Bridge is where the VIPs sit over the track. You'll learn that this is the world's fastest 1-mile track, with straightaways at 9 degrees and turns banked at 24 degrees. According to NASCAR drivers, the sensation of speed is like nothing anywhere else. With a 22-second lap, they travel the length of a football field in 1 second.

You also get to see some of the race cars and to stand on the track. It's amazing to be there looking up at all those seats.

For another unique tour, change gears from thinking about cars to thinking about planes. Nearby Dover Air Force Base (DAFB) is an active military base, so it's off-limits to the public. However, there's a wonderful museum next to the base that visitors can tour—the **Air Mobility Command (AMC) Museum**. Visitors enter the museum from an entrance separate from the base.

To get there from Dover Downs Hotel & Casino, turn left onto US 13 South. Stay to the left on South Bay Road and merge onto DE 1. Take exit 91 and turn left onto DE 9. Make a left at the museum entrance, which is on Heritage Road.

An intriguing, one-of-a-kind museum, the AMC Museum has volunteer guides, some of whom are retired military, with fascinating stories.

Even if you're not a plane enthusiast, you'll enjoy this air museum's exhibits. One is a retired Air Force Two, the type of plane used by the US vice president. For many, this is as close as you can get to the lifestyle of the vice president when he travels by jet.

Air Force Two is actually smaller than one might expect, but it's interesting nonetheless. Like taking a tour of the White House, seeing Air Force Two, even a retired version, brings us that much closer to a seat of power.

Visitors can also look at real-life bombers, cargo planes, tankers, and fighters—some from World War II and others more recent. The fact that the museum is next to an active air base makes spending time here extra special. From the museum, you can even watch flights taking off and landing at the base.

When heading home, take DE 8 West to MD 311 South to MD 480 West. Turn right onto MD 404 West and continue onto US 50 West and the Chesapeake Bay Bridge.

IN THE AREA

Delmar, Maryland/Delaware

Attractions and Recreation

PUBLIC PARK, at North Penn Avenue and East State Street.

Dover, Delaware

Accommodations

DOVER DOWNS HOTEL & CASINO. Call 302-674-4600 or 1-800-711-5882. Website: www.doverdowns.com.

Attractions and Recreation

AIR MOBILITY COMMAND (AMC) MUSEUM. Call 302-677-5938. Website: www.amcmuseum.org.

DOVER INTERNATIONAL SPEEDWAY. Call 302-883-6500 or 1-800-441-7223. Website: www.doverspeedway.com.

FIFER ORCHARDS FARM & COUNTRY STORE, Camden-Wyoming. Call 302-697-2141. Website: www.fiferorchards.com.

Dining/Drinks

COOL SPRINGS FISH BAR & RESTAURANT. Call 302-698-1955. Website: www.coolspringsfishbar.com.

MICHELE'S AT DOVER DOWNS. Call 302-857-2120. Website: www.dover downs.com/dining/restaurants/Micheles.

Easton, Maryland

Accommodations

TIDEWATER INN. Call 410-822-1300 or 1-800-237-8775 (reservations). Website: www.tidewaterinn.com.

Attractions and Recreation

RAILROAD DEPOT.

Dining/Drinks

HILL'S CAFÉ & JUICE BAR, inside Hill's Drug Store. Call 410-822-9751. Website: hillscafeandjuicebar.com.

OUT OF THE FIRE. Call 410-770-4777. Website: www.outofthefire.com.

Ridgely, Maryland

Attractions and Recreation

ANNUAL STRAWBERRY FESTIVAL, held in May.

RAILROAD MEMORIAL PARK.

Dining/Drinks

RIDGELY PHARMACY & ICE CREAM PARLOR. Call 410-634-9800. Website: visitcaroline.org/listings/ridgely-pharmacy-ice-cream-parlor-cafe.

5

ISLAND-HOPPING ON THE VIRGINIA EASTERN SHORE

ESTIMATED LENGTH: 480 miles round-trip from the Chesapeake Bay Bridge, plus about 24 nautical miles to and from Tangier Island

ESTIMATED TIME: 3–4 days (You could spend a summer here, but a long weekend will give you a taste, and you'll get to know the area well enough that you can plan a return visit.)

GETTING THERE: From Annapolis, take US 50 East across the Chesapeake Bay Bridge and continue on US 50 East toward Ocean City. At Salisbury, head south on US 13 past Pocomoke City and into Virginia. Then take VA 175 East onto Chincoteague Island. It's about a three-hour drive, without detours, from the Bay Bridge to Chincoteague. From Salisbury, it takes less than an hour to Chincoteague.

From Norfolk, Virginia, or Virginia Beach, take Northampton Boulevard/US 13 North across the Chesapeake Bay Bridge–Tunnel (different from the Chesapeake Bay Bridge) to Cape Charles and reverse the order of this trip.

HIGHLIGHTS: Isolated and obscure natural beauty; Chesapeake Bay Bridge–Tunnel; Tangier Island with isolated culture and a special form of the English language; Chincoteague with wild ponies, dolphins, and birding; former steamboat landing in Cape Charles; town of Onancock; Exmore Diner.

This trip takes place on the **Virginia Eastern Shore**, a part of the Commonwealth of Virginia that is often forgotten. Kids will love the outdoors and wildlife; adults will love the romantic nature of the waterfronts and the delightful quiet in the sparsely populated countryside.

Many people know that **Assateague** is partially in Maryland and partially in Virginia and that the Virginia section is adjacent to **Chincoteague**, where

CHINCOTEAGUE PONIES IN A HUDDLE TERESA A. BALLARD

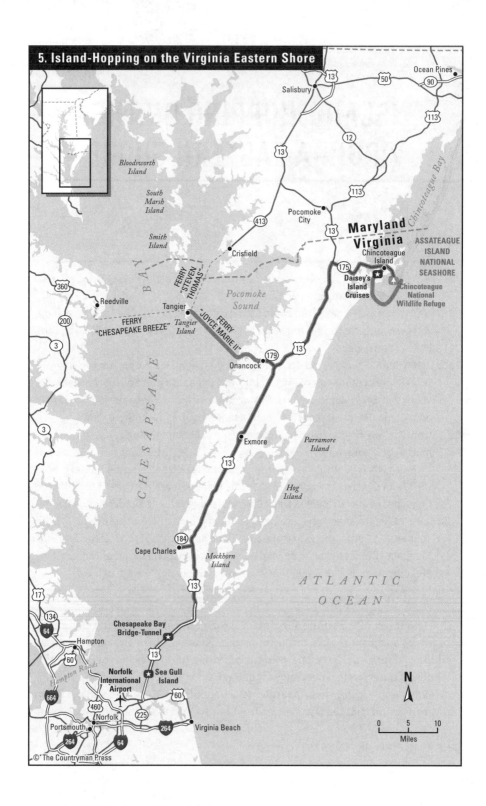

Ocean Pines

Salisbury

Bloodsworth
Island

South
Marsh
Island

Smith
Island

Pocomoke
City

Crisfield

Maryland
Virginia

Chincoteague
Island

ASSATEAGUE
ISLAND
NATIONAL
SEASHORE

Chincoteague Bay

FERRY
"STEVEN
THOMAS"

Daisey's
Island
Cruises

Chincoteague
National
Wildlife Refuge

Reedville

Tangier

Pocomoke
Sound

FERRY
"CHESAPEAKE BREEZE"

Tangier
Island

FERRY
"JOYCE MARIE II"

Onancock

B
A
Y

Exmore

Parramore
Island

Hog
Island

C H E S A P E A K E

Cape Charles

Mockhorn
Island

A T L A N T I C

O C E A N

Chesapeake Bay
Bridge-Tunnel

Hampton

Hampton Roads

Norfolk
International
Airport

Sea Gull
Island

N

Norfolk

Portsmouth

Virginia Beach

0   5   10
Miles

© The Countryman Press

there are wild ponies herded across the channel in an organized swim every summer. However, most people do not know how much there is to see on the Virginia Eastern Shore, which is 70 miles long and utterly charming. Maryland may try to keep the Virginia side a secret, but apparently Virginia used to keep it a sort-of secret too; many Virginia maps didn't include the area until recently.

This itinerary is out of the ordinary and promises to be memorable. Even if you fill the days with lots of activities, it will be relaxing. Of course, there are low-lying areas, so avoid going during a nor'easter or hurricane, although that's true for just about all the trips in this book. And unless you love crowds, you might want to avoid the annual Chincoteague pony swim in July, when tens of thousands of people come to watch.

Before planning a trip to a remote area like the Virginia Eastern Shore, it's best to speak with some locals, to be prepared.

One way of doing that is to talk to the owners of a B&B where you plan to stay. That's how you learn the local color, the layout of the area, and details you might not find out otherwise.

For instance, there's the ongoing possibility of high winds. One local tells a story about his experience: "It was windy, and we went out in kayaks. The wind was so strong, it almost blew us to Ocean City." He was referring to Ocean City, Maryland, about 50 miles north along the Atlantic Ocean. If you're not a strong kayaker, or even if you are, this information is important.

Two lovely B&Bs where the owners give you insights into the local landscape are the **Channel Bass Inn** in Chincoteague and **The Inn at Onancock** in Onancock. If you're planning to spend a weekend, you might stay at either B&B for both nights or stay in one for one night and the other for the next night.

Take US 13 South from Salisbury (or US 13 North from Norfolk/Virginia Beach if you're reversing the trip). After you cross into Virginia from the north, turn left onto VA 175 East and travel about 10 miles toward Chincoteague.

This route takes you on a dramatic causeway across marshes and wetlands. (A causeway is a road raised up on an embankment to cross a broad body of water or wetlands.) Once you cross the drawbridge that goes over Chincoteague Channel, you'll be on Chincoteague Island. Turn right at the stoplight onto Main Street.

Follow Main Street about 5 blocks, then turn left onto Church Street. The Channel Bass Inn is on the right. (If the inn is booked, there are other B&Bs and hotels on the island including a **Hampton Inn & Suites**.) Check in and then park around back. After you get settled into your room, you're ready to start your adventure.

Centuries ago, a Native American tribe led by Chief Barabokees and

Emperor Waskawampe claimed the island as their home, naming it Chincoteague, which means "beautiful land across the water."

The first stop on your journey to view this lovely land is **Chincoteague National Wildlife Refuge** on Assateague Island. To get there, go back on Main Street toward the stoplight at the drawbridge. Turn right onto Maddox Boulevard (VA 175 East) and follow the road for a few miles, crossing Assateague Channel.

At the wildlife refuge, stop at the entrance, where you need to pay the per-car fee and buy a map to guide you. There's a lovely Atlantic Ocean beach in the refuge; unlike many other Atlantic beaches, this one is without condos or other commercial structures to compete with the natural beauty. A 0.25-mile path (Lighthouse Trail) leads from a parking lot to the 1867 **Assateague Lighthouse**; you can climb up into the lighthouse if it's open (generally April through November). There are also several other trails you can take by car or on foot.

The refuge is on the Atlantic Flyway, so bird lovers delight in visiting during the spring and fall migrations, when more than 300 species of birds stop over. Herons and egrets are among the many prevalent species.

Naturally, you'll want to bring sunscreen. But also vital to your comfort is bug spray, preferably with a high concentration of DEET, if you can tolerate it without an allergic reaction. Between mosquitoes and no-see-ums, you'll absolutely need a lot of bug spray.

Don't worry if you don't see the wild ponies for which Chincoteague is so famous. You'll cover that later when you take a sunset cruise. If you do come across some ponies up close and personal, it's important to remember they are wild animals. Although they appear tame, don't feed or pet them as they may kick or bite.

On your way off Assateague, keep watch for the **Museum of Chincoteague Island** on Maddox Boulevard on your right. There's a small admission fee, but it's worth a visit to get a feel for the history of the area. For homemade ice cream, **Island Creamery** is also on Maddox, not far from the museum.

If you get back in time, the Channel Bass Inn offers a traditional British afternoon tea. Then you can grab a sweater or jacket and head back to Main Street, turning left from the inn. Travel about 1.5 miles south of downtown Chincoteague and look for a blue metal roof on your right. That's **Daisey's Island Cruises**, which offers pontoon boat excursions. Make reservations in advance to make sure you can get out on the water.

This boat trip is wonderfully comfortable; with a maximum of only six people, there's lots of room for observing wildlife. If the weather and season are right, you'll likely see dolphins, assorted birds, a deer or two, and a group of wild ponies grazing on the shore.

The two-hour cruise covers Chincoteague Inlet and the southernmost tip, or "Hook," of Assateague Island, plus Tom's Cove. The sunset is sure to be beautiful, and the quality of the guides is excellent.

There are other island boat tour companies, so if Daisey's cannot accommodate you, ask the B&B owner for other recommendations.

As for the ponies, they are said to be descended from horses brought over on a Spanish ship that was wrecked offshore in the 1600s. Legend has it that the horses swam to safety, and the wild ponies today are their descendants.

After the cruise, go directly to **Bill's Prime Seafood & Steaks**, which is on the right-hand side of Main Street as you drive back into town. The restaurant is not open too late, so make a reservation early in the day so they know to expect you. The seafood there is typical of the region—well-conceived and well-prepared.

Get up early the next day and have a lovely breakfast at the inn. Then get in your car and head west on VA 175 back across the drawbridge. Turn left onto US 13 South and travel about 15 or 20 miles to the town of Onley. Turn right onto VA 179 (West Main Street) and drive about 1.5 miles until the street ends at the harbor in the small town of **Onancock**.

Park your car. If you plan in advance, you should try to make a reservation for the 10 a.m. **Tangier-Onancock Ferry** on the *Joyce Marie II*. Like nearby Smith Island, Tangier is too remote and too far from land for a bridge, so boats are the primary mode of transportation to and from the island. Smith Island is accessible only by boat, but Tangier also has a tiny airstrip that allows small private planes to land.

On Tangier, most of the men make their living from fishing and crabbing in the bay. During warm weather, tourism also plays an important role in the economic viability of the island.

Arrive 15 or 20 minutes early for the 10 a.m. ferry, which takes about an hour and 15 minutes to reach Tangier Harbor. The ferry holds only about two dozen people, so it's best to make a reservation and even call a second time to confirm. After coming all this way, you'd hate to be left on the dock for lack of room.

Besides the ferry from Onancock, there are alternate ferries to Tangier: the **Steven Thomas** from Crisfield on Maryland's Eastern Shore and the **Chesapeake Breeze** from Reedville on Virginia's Western Shore. These ferries are larger, holding upwards of 300 people each. Taking one of them provides a more touristy experience; however, reservations are generally not necessary on the bigger boats. Of course, it never hurts to have a reservation.

Tangier is a fascinating island populated by families who have lived on the island for generations. Like their Smith Island counterparts, their speech is a dialect similar to old Elizabethan English. Also like Smith Islanders, residents are generally active in the crabbing and fishing trades.

A British fleet used Tangier as its headquarters in 1814 with the intent of ravaging the Chesapeake during the War of 1812. Thousands of British troops sailed up the bay from the island to their failed attack on Baltimore's Fort McHenry. It was during that attack that Francis Scott Key wrote "The Star-Spangled Banner."

Tangier Island belongs to Virginia, but it is so close to Crisfield on the mainland in Maryland that many Tangier residents keep cars in Crisfield. From there, they do their shopping and errands, usually in the Salisbury area.

If you want to stay over on Tangier, there are a few B&Bs on the island, but you should definitely book in advance. Otherwise, you really can see most of the island in the approximately four hours before the ferry leaves to return to Onancock.

If you don't have overnight reservations, make sure not to miss the ferry, which leaves Tangier at 3:30 p.m. and arrives back in Onancock around 4:45 p.m. Other than the public ferries, your only other option is to charter a boat or possibly a plane from the tiny airstrip on the west side of the island.

There are no traffic lights and only about 15 to 20 cars and pickup trucks on Tangier. The island is tiny—only 3 miles by 1 mile—so usual methods of transportation are by foot, golf cart, or bike. You can rent a golf cart or bike in town about a block or two from the ferry dock. The golf carts are easy to drive, with just on-off and forward-reverse options.

Tangier is a charming, isolated place with expansive views, where you can see birds migrating, go fishing, explore by kayak, and generally chill

TANGIER ISLAND WITH GOLF CART TRANSPORT

out. There's not much else to do. "We see the bay every day," one lifelong resident explains. "And so we tell each other yarnies." That's tall tales to the rest of us, pronounced *yar-knees*.

And yet, compared with nearby Smith Island, also in the middle of the bay, Tangier is more commercial, more cognizant of catering to tourists by selling food and renting bikes and golf carts to the boatloads of visitors who come to see what's there. You can get lunch at several places. It's also worth a half hour of your time to tour the **Tangier History Museum and Interpretive Cultural Center** to learn more about the history and people of the island.

Stop in at the post office to chat with the postmaster, or go to **Daley & Son Grocery**, the only grocery store on the island, to get a glimpse of what life on this isolated island is like. Fresh vegetables and meat get delivered once a week, on Thursdays, so the store is crowded that day.

Be patient when talking with residents of Tangier. Their Elizabethan style of speech is a bit hard to understand. You'll have to listen closely and will likely have to ask them to repeat something more than once.

There are generators on the island, and there's also an underwater cable connecting Tangier with the electric grid. There are also, of course, crab shanties and docks—lots of docks. And if you walk along the beach outside town, you may find some sea glass.

After the return ferry ride, which is a pleasurable trip out on the bay, you'll arrive back in Onancock. From the ferry dock, you're only about three blocks from The Inn at Onancock on North Street. This is a lovely inn with comfortable rooms, gracious hosts, spa-style baths, and a relaxed atmosphere. For dinner, try the restaurant at the **Charlotte Hotel**, just a few blocks from the B&B.

The next morning, set aside a little time to drive around the town of Onancock (pronounced *oh-NAN-cock*), a takeoff on its original Native American name, Owanancock, meaning "foggy place."

To head farther south, drive back to US 13 and turn right onto US 13 South. Turn right onto VA 184 West, about 10 miles before the Chesapeake Bay Bridge–Tunnel. Stay on VA 184 about 2 miles, and you'll pass the town of Cape Charles's water tower, which is designed to look like a lighthouse.

In 1884, the railroad was extended from Pocomoke City in Maryland to **Cape Charles**. This proved to be a boon to the town, and residents quickly built some beautiful Victorian houses, many of which still stand today.

Cape Charles was once teeming with activity when the steamboats docked there. Now the harbor is filled with yachts. There's also a tiny public bay beach where you might find sea glass, and there are cute little shops in town.

Cape Charles was actually founded by a railroad (the New York, Philadelphia and Norfolk Railroad) and a ferry company in 1884. Until 1948, the

TANGIER ISLAND LANDSCAPE

town was the ferry departure point for steamboat traffic heading across the bay to Norfolk.

Cape Charles lost the passenger rail and steamboat ferry lines. Now rail service for freight is gone too.

From Cape Charles, turn around and go back to continue taking US 13 South. You'll soon come to the tollbooths for the **Chesapeake Bay Bridge–Tunnel**. The bridge-tunnel is more than 17 miles long across the Chesapeake Bay from the tip of the Eastern Shore to Virginia Beach—17.6 miles from shore to shore, to be exact. It's a bridge with two 1-mile tunnels that allow ships to pass above without having drawbridge or height issues.

The officially named Lucius J. Kellam, Jr. Bridge–Tunnel opened in 1964 and is still considered an engineering feat, heralded globally. Engineering students and many others from around the world often visit to see it firsthand.

Nearly four million vehicles cross this one-of-a-kind structure annually. Designated one of the seven engineering wonders of the modern world in 1965 and considered the largest bridge-tunnel complex in the United States, it's simply amazing. The "big ships"—the giant cargo and other ships—need to cross one or both of the two major shipping channels into and out of the bay—the Chesapeake Channel and the Thimble Shoal Channel.

Going south from Cape Charles, the first tunnel allows ships to travel from the Atlantic Ocean north to Baltimore and other destinations beyond the Chesapeake Channel.

The second, more southern tunnel is for the shipping lane that heads from the Atlantic Ocean to the Chesapeake Bay and then to Norfolk and Hampton Roads, Virginia, this time in the Thimble Shoal Channel. A parallel tunnel is currently under construction in Thimble Shoal Channel to increase the number of lanes. Completion of the new tunnel is scheduled for 2023.

Four man-made islands were constructed as part of the bridge-tunnel; there's one on each end of the two tunnels. Of the four, **Sea Gull Island** is the man-made island closest to Norfolk and Virginia Beach. It used to have a fishing pier constructed from leftover sections of bridge materials—a pier that gave fishermen (and women) the chance to fish 3.5 miles out in the bay without getting on a boat.

In beautiful, sunny weather, fishing from this 625-foot pier in the middle of the bay was a lovely way to spend a day. There was a restaurant overlooking the fishing pier, too, and you could park on the bridge to dine and enjoy the view. But the tunnel expansion unfortunately eliminated the possibility of doing this. The restaurant and gift shop are now permanently closed, but luckily the fishing pier is scheduled to be renovated and reopened in 2023.

If you're fearful of the drive across the bridge-tunnel, you can call 757-331-2960 in advance to make arrangements for an employee to drive you and your vehicle across. You still pay the toll, but there's no additional charge for this service.

Regarding weather concerns, bridge-tunnel personnel monitor the conditions constantly. You can check on wind restrictions and other potential travel delays by calling 757-331-2960 or going to the website at www.cbbt .com; click on "Travel Information" and then "Weather." From the website, you can also download an MP3 driving tour from the "Activities" section.

For birdwatchers, the bridge is directly in the fall and winter south migratory flyway. Birds seeking refuge from nasty weather can generally be seen on the safe havens created by the man-made islands in the bridge-tunnel complex, which are generally not accessible to visitors.

From the roadway, passengers may see dolphins, which appear occasionally, but will not be as likely to see whales.

For ship lovers, the waters around the bridge-tunnel contain a veritable cornucopia of boats. With the US Navy at Norfolk and major urban centers nearby, both military ships and huge commercial "floating Walmarts" with all sorts of goods on board can be seen coming and going.

The bridge-tunnel is a direct route from Virginia Beach to Virginia's Eastern Shore. The Chesapeake Bay is on the west side, the Atlantic Ocean on the east. It's an engineering marvel and a travel convenience that saves motorists 90 miles or more. From wildlife to ships, it provides a constantly changing horizon.

If you're the curious type, you can drive all the way to the Virginia Beach side of the bridge-tunnel and pay a second toll to turn around and come back—just for the experience of it. Or you can reverse the trip if you're start-ing out near Norfolk. (The return toll is reduced if you come back within 24 hours and use E-ZPass). As you travel north from the bridge-tunnel, take US 13 (Lankford Highway) on the way back to Salisbury, Maryland, and the Chesapeake Bay Bridge. There's one more stop to make while still on Virgin-ia's Eastern Shore. At the Royal Farms convenience store in **Exmore**, turn right at the stoplight and then left at the stop sign.

Drive about half a mile. On the left you'll reach the **Exmore Diner**, offer-ing fabulous comfort food at low prices with lots of down-home atmosphere. They serve breakfast all day if they're not busy, except for waffles after a certain time. Seating is at the counter or in booths.

The diner is in a converted railcar brought to Exmore from New Jersey in 1954 by the diner's first owner. It is frequented by a crowd of locals, who will look up for a moment at a stranger and then nonchalantly go back to eating their meals.

If you talk to the locals, they'll readily tell you about the "come-heres"—those

TANGIER ISLAND

who moved here from somewhere else—and the "from-heres" or "born-heres"—everyone born in and around Exmore and proud of it.

After a quick but satisfying meal (or take-out if you're not hungry but want to try the diner's food), turn left out of the parking lot and then turn right onto US 13 North.

You could take a year to really get to know the Virginia Eastern Shore, but on this journey, you've gotten a good start.

IN THE AREA

Cape Charles

Attractions and Recreation

CHESAPEAKE BAY BRIDGE–TUNNEL. Call 757-331-2960. Website: www.cbbt.com.

Chincoteague

Accommodations

CHANNEL BASS INN. Call 757-336-6148. Website: www.channelbassinn.com.

HAMPTON INN & SUITES. Call 757-336-1616. Website: www.hamptoninnchincoteague.com.

Attractions and Recreation

ASSATEAGUE LIGHTHOUSE. Website: www.assateagueisland.com/lighthouse/lighthouse_info.htm.

CHINCOTEAGUE NATIONAL WILDLIFE REFUGE. Call 757-336-6122. Website: www.fws.gov/refuge/chincoteague.

DAISEY'S ISLAND CRUISES. Call 757-336-5556. Website: www.daiseysislandcruises.com.

MUSEUM OF CHINCOTEAGUE ISLAND. Call 757-336-6117. Website: www.chincoteaguemuseum.com.

Dining/Drinks

BILL'S PRIME SEAFOOD & STEAKS. Call 757-336-5831. Website: www.bills seafoodrestaurant.com.

ISLAND CREAMERY. Call 757-336-6236. Website: www.islandcreamery.net.

Exmore

Dining/Drinks

EXMORE DINER. Call 757-442-2313. Website: www.exmoredinerva.com.

Onancock

Accommodations

THE INN AT ONANCOCK. Call 757-789-7711. Website: www.innatonancock .com.

Attractions and Recreation

TANGIER-ONANCOCK FERRY, with Captain Mark Crockett, *Joyce Marie II.* Call 757-891-2505. Website: www.tangierisland-va.com/tangier boat or www.tangierferry.com.

Dining/Drinks

CHARLOTTE HOTEL & RESTAURANT. Call 757-787-7400. Website: www .thecharlottehotel.com.

Tangier Island

Attractions and Recreation

CHESAPEAKE BREEZE **(TANGIER CRUISES),** out of Reedville. Call 804-453-2628. Website: www.tangiercruise.com.

DALEY & SON GROCERY. Call 757-891-2469.

STEVEN THOMAS (**TANGIER ISLAND CRUISES**), out of Crisfield, MD. Call 410-968-2338. Website: www.tangierislandcruises.com.

TANGIER HISTORY MUSEUM AND INTERPRETIVE CULTURAL CENTER. Call 757-891-2374. Website: www.findyourchesapeake.com/places/tangier -history-museum-and-interpretive-cultural-center.

6

TOURING QUINTESSENTIAL ATLANTIC BEACHES

ESTIMATED LENGTH: 240 miles round-trip from the Chesapeake Bay Bridge

ESTIMATED TIME: 3–4 days

GETTING THERE: From Annapolis, go to Kent Island across the Chesapeake Bay Bridge—a 4.3-mile span that takes only a few minutes at the 50-mile-an-hour speed limit. The bridge operates year-round, and there are two spans side by side—one for each direction, although sometimes with heavy traffic or repairs, the westbound bridge is used for two-way traffic. To Ocean City, take US 50 East. To the Delaware beaches, take US 50 East to MD 404 East.

From Norfolk, Virginia, or Virginia Beach, take the Chesapeake Bay Bridge–Tunnel, a 17.6-mile span that takes about a half hour each way. From the bridge-tunnel, take US 13 North to US 113 North to US 50 East to MD 528 North.

From Philadelphia, take I-95 South to DE 1 South. DE 1 runs north and south throughout Delaware and turns into the Coastal Highway through Ocean City, Maryland.

HIGHLIGHTS: The scents and sounds of a quintessential beach vacation, adventure in the sand and surf, excitement at the bars and restaurants, relaxation and quiet on deserted sections of beach, Fenwick Island Lighthouse, the iconic Ocean City boardwalk.

Salt water is evocative, refreshing, and healing, especially when the warmth of the sun embraces us. There's magic inherent in the salt water drops left on our skin from frolicking in the waves, and year-round, the sound of the waves relaxes us. An ocean visit also calls up memories of time spent on beaches long ago. So it's no secret that going to the ocean is great for unwinding,

ART IN REHOBOTH BEACH

destressing, and reconnecting with ourselves, our significant others, and our families.

For this itinerary, we're going to visit Ocean City, Maryland, and the Southern Delaware beaches along the Atlantic Ocean. There are beaches elsewhere on the ocean and along rivers and bays. But for this particular journey, we'll concentrate on the 30 or so miles up and down the Atlantic Ocean between Rehoboth Beach, Delaware, and Ocean City.

In Maryland, Delaware, and Washington, DC, all roads in the summer lead not to Rome but seemingly to these Atlantic beaches in a quest for the smell of salt water, the feel of hot sun on the sand beneath your feet, and the cooling waves of the surf. You can explore all these beaches in a few days. Or you can pick one beach and stay put, enjoying the ambience.

The coastline is ever changing, ever evolving. Erosion, beach

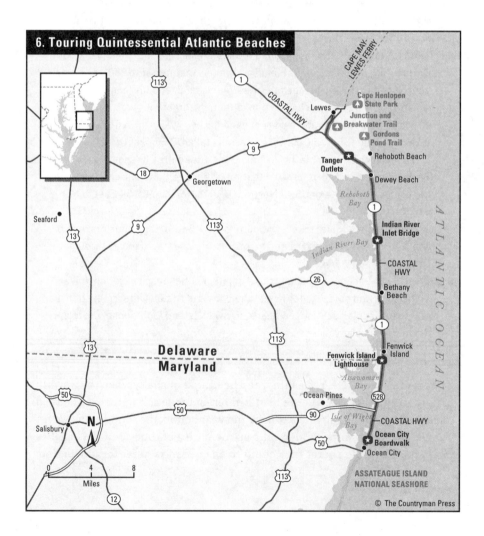

replenishment, storms, fires, the power of the water and the tides, and time all play a part. Politicians, community leaders, and developers figure into the mix with competing motivations and desires.

Where one community seeks to restore rather than rebuild, another chooses development and higher population densities. This keeps the landscape interesting and in flux as the surrounding waters ebb and flow.

The name **Ocean City** brings forth images of sand and bikinis, salt water and people-watching, junk food on the boardwalk, and early-morning bike rides. For those who grew up in Maryland or moved there from other places, Ocean City is "going down the ocean." It is *the* place for playing in the waves, walking on the beach while dipping your feet in the water, searching for seashells, and getting a tan.

It has a fabulous 2.5-mile boardwalk complete with amusements of various kinds, from rides to an instant photo machine; food indulgences like ice cream and French fries; and shops selling inexpensive T-shirts, flip-flops, and souvenirs.

Ocean City is long and narrow, with the Atlantic Ocean on one side and two bays—Isle of Wight and Assawoman—on the other. It stretches for 10 miles from its southern inlet to the edge of Fenwick Island at the Delaware state line. Major hurricanes and other storms sometimes cause extensive flooding since the city is surrounded by water on three sides.

Summer is high season, and to say that Ocean City is crowded then is an understatement. Some hotels require a minimum number of nights, and it's best to have reservations.

One cannot have grown up along the Mid-Atlantic without being likely to have fond childhood memories of vacations in Ocean City or on the Southern Delaware beaches.

Interestingly, residents from the Washington, DC, area tend to gravitate to Rehoboth, Dewey, and Bethany Beaches in Delaware, while those from Baltimore and Maryland's Eastern Shore traditionally head to Ocean City.

Each beach town has its own personality, its own quirks and unique flavor. All have similar weather, sand that gets hot in the summer sun, and beach food such as saltwater taffy, ice cream, and pizza. There are motels and hotels and B&Bs, as well as condos for rent through management companies.

There's an enticing sunrise over the ocean. You can rent bikes and ride on a boardwalk in the early morning during summer, or bring your own bike and ride any time of day in the off-season. There are also waves and seashells, and birds that congregate late in the day.

Ocean City is Maryland's sole ocean beach; it swells in population during the warm months and shrinks again to strictly year-round residents when the weather is cold. It is a stereotypical beach town with an abundance of amusements, miniature golf, greasy fries, ice cream, and suntan lotion. You can find plenty of joints serving seafood, pizza, and burgers—all the usual beach foods.

A Monolithic Structure

The Chesapeake Bay Bridge is a major deal. It changed commerce in towns up and down the bay—those with boat landings often faded, while those near the bridge flourished. It made the Eastern Shore more accessible, contributing to the Western Shore getting less attention from vacationers bent on reaching the Atlantic Ocean.

Driving from Baltimore to Ocean City takes about 4 hours now without stopping—certainly a doable drive even for a weekend.

But according to some travelers, the Chesapeake Bay Bridge is scary. At one time, the Maryland Transportation Authority (MDTA) offered rides to those afraid to drive their own vehicles across it. The state discontinued this service, but there's a private company, **Kent Island Express**, that does Bay Bridge drive-overs for a fee; you meet them by the bridge, and they drive your vehicle across with you in it.

Why is this bridge so adored and yet so feared? Winds can shut down the bridge when conditions make it too dangerous. And the weather around the bridge can change on a dime, frightening drivers with its sometimes-sudden intensity.

The barricades are only about a little under 4 feet tall, so there have been accidents in which cars have gone over the side. Some worry because there is no place to pull over in an emergency. Occasionally people have panic attacks and fear getting sick or passing out while crossing the bridge.

DOUBLE SPAN OF THE CHESAPEAKE BAY BRIDGE

Officially known as the William Preston Lane, Jr. Memorial Bridge, the bridge is 200 feet high in places; and while there are longer bridges, 4.3 miles is nothing to sneeze at. There are two parallel spans—one constructed in 1952, the other in 1973. The eastbound span is only two lanes wide, so there's no middle lane for skittish drivers to use.

The westbound span has three lanes, but if there's heavy traffic going eastbound, the MDTA often changes the direction in one of the three lanes to ease eastbound traffic. When this happens, the westbound span becomes two-way, adding to some drivers' stress.

There's talk that the spans are functionally obsolete and need to be replaced. There's also talk about constructing another separate Bay Bridge in a different location. But either option would constitute an expensive, long-term project. For the time being, this is it.

Yet the two spans are beautiful and ultimately convenient as they unite the eastern and western sides of the bay. At the 50-mile-an-hour speed limit, it takes about five minutes to cross, so it's a quick trip.

There's a toll eastbound but none westbound. If you are really fearful, you can always drive around the northern end of the bay and then back down the opposite shore—like they did in the old days.

For more upscale dining, **Fager's Island** is a perennial bayside favorite for dinner with a lively bar nightlife afterward; the restaurant also has an excellent Sunday brunch. **The Angler**, located by the "Route 50 bridge" into town, is also a good option. With the purchase of a lunch or dinner entrée, you can take a 45-minute scenic cruise for a minimal charge.

To dine while looking out over the docks where commercial fishing boats are moored, try **Shark on the Harbor** in West Ocean City. And across the street is **Sunset Grille**, also focusing on seafood; there's often music in the evening as well as outside dining.

And then there is Southern Delaware.

Perhaps to some, a beach is a beach is a beach—but not really. There's the particular boardwalk to consider, and whether there are single-family beach houses or condo high-rises. There are the winds and wildlife—whether birds are of interest to you or wild ponies descended from Spanish horses that survived a shipwreck.

There are rocks and the tides, fishing and crabbing nearby. So much goes into choosing a beach, for each beach has a different vibe.

There are the year-round residents and the places the visitors come from to keep in mind. There are the amusements besides the natural ones of sun and sand. And there is the food, the fishing, the sailing, the kayaking, and the bird-watching.

ONE OF MANY ENTRANCES TO THE BOARDWALK IN OCEAN CITY

When it comes to a boardwalk, some people think, the bigger the better. So you'll definitely want to walk or bike (early in the morning) the 2.5-mile Ocean City boardwalk. Pleasures along this and most seaside boardwalks include food and drink, games, and the ultimate people-watching, from flimsy bathing suits to unusual behavior.

In the summertime, especially on weekends, you can expect to run into bumper-to-bumper traffic in many areas. Take a deep breath and relax. You can't fight it. However, you should plan to travel at off-times whenever possible, such as early Friday or Monday morning, instead of Friday night, Saturday morning, or Sunday night.

There will also likely be crowds at the major beaches and lines at popular restaurants. Going on the beach right after a large storm will probably afford you some solitude, although the treasure seekers will be out and about searching for valuables spit up by the sea.

Shoulder seasons—just before Memorial Day and after Labor Day—are really the loveliest times. The weather is still warm, and the crowds are gone.

Obviously, some of the small inland towns and bay beaches are less crowded than the ocean shore. And if the crowds get to you, that's the time to go off and explore an obscure museum or do some outlet shopping.

After exploring Ocean City, you should also check out the Delaware beaches. Rehoboth Beach is rather upscale, with many year-round residents and superb restaurants, like **The Cultured Pearl** and **Chesapeake & Maine**. And you can't go wrong when you're staying at either the **Boardwalk Plaza Hotel** or **The Bellmoor Inn & Spa**.

Dewey Beach is a seasonal party town with lots of nighttime bars and live entertainment catering to the college and younger crowds. Dewey Beach is also the East Coast capital of skimboarding—a hybrid between skateboarding and surfboarding. Family-oriented events and activities, like movies and bonfires on the beach, also take place as families are joining the college kids in flocking to the beachside town.

Bethany Beach is most famous for its expansive condos and rentals.

Fenwick Island is right on the Delaware border with Maryland. It has the iconic **Fenwick Island Lighthouse** and is quieter than the other beaches.

All these beaches provide the essence of the summer beach experience—sand, sun, casual attire, relaxation, and fun. While the trappings are similar, each beach has its own ambience.

Happily, there is no sales tax in Delaware. Tax-free shopping and dining really make a difference to the budget when you're on a two- or three-day holiday. Add to that the preponderance of large outlet centers on the Coastal Highway in Rehoboth Beach, as well as small boutiques in downtown Rehoboth Beach, and you've got a winning combination off-season and in stormy weather.

Jughandle

The first time you see a jughandle sign, you'll likely do a double take. Unless you're from New Jersey, of course, in which case you'll get it: It's a turn that's also known as a Jersey left. (The term "Jersey left" can also mean an abrupt left at the beginning of a green light—not what we're talking about here.)

A jughandle is an indirect way to make a left turn, where you have to loop to the right when where you really want to go is left.

The New Jersey state government has considered banning all future jughandles, so their ultimate fate is undetermined. Their history, however, is immortalized. The jughandle traffic pattern was started in the 1940s to help control traffic. By 1960, New Jersey had 160 jughandles.

Some people love them, and some people hate them.

Delaware has adopted one, right where US 9 East (Lewes-Georgetown Highway) runs into DE 1 (to go north, where a left-hand turn is needed). There's signage that warns about the upcoming jughandle, calling it by name. Of course, not everyone knows what the sign means.

There are three general types of jughandles, but that's really getting into the weeds. This is enough information for you to know what it means when you see JUGHANDLE up ahead.

Just don't get excited and think, *It's a jughandle—I must be in New Jersey.* You may actually be in Delaware, on your way to the beach.

There are outlet stores outside Ocean City too, as well as in Queenstown right after you cross the Bay Bridge, but those outlets are in Maryland, which has a sales tax.

Even if you're staying in Ocean City, it's worthwhile taking a ride up the Coastal Highway into Rehoboth Beach for a major shopping trip to **Tanger Outlets**. They are right on DE 1 in three separate outdoor centers (Midway, Seaside, and Bayside), so they are easy to find. No sales tax plus outlet malls equals bargain hunting for everyone so inclined.

At meals, it also makes a difference when you get the restaurant bill and there's no tax added, especially when you're used to paying tax elsewhere.

With many possible activities, nothing quite beats walking on the beach. But there is much to do beyond the beaches as well. There are bike rentals all over, or you can bring your own bike. The **Junction and Breakwater Trail** is 6 miles one way between Lewes and Rehoboth Beach; this former rail trail is great for biking and hiking. The 5.2-mile **Gordons Pond Trail** in Cape Henlopen State Park links Lewes and Rehoboth too.

There's also kayaking, waterskiing, and stand-up paddling. If you want to fish, you can rent a charter (where the whole boat is yours, besides the crew of course). Or you can go on a "head boat," where you pay per person (or by head) and will likely be on board with other paying customers. Deep-sea fishing, fly-fishing, dock fishing, surf fishing, fresh- or saltwater fishing . . . you can find it all. For information on the various types of fishing available, consult **Delaware Surf Fishing** or the **Delaware Division of Fish & Wildlife**.

There are plenty of public golf courses and mini-golf too, plus rides, games, and amusements.

If your idea of heaven is reading a book from a chair or blanket on the beach while smelling salt air and listening to ocean waves, there are two outstanding bookstores in Southern Delaware right by the beaches. **Browseabout Books** is in Rehoboth and **Bethany Beach Books** is in, you guessed it, Bethany Beach.

Though you might like to wing it rather than planning ahead, you'll find that's not a practical approach when you're headed to these beaches. During high season (Memorial Day to Labor Day), there are events and concerts on weekends, as well as a mass of sun worshipers from Philadelphia, Wilmington, Baltimore, and Washington, DC. Therefore, it's wise to have advance lodging reservations.

During shoulder seasons, as well as in the winter, you run the risk that places you want to stay may be closed or open only limited dates. This is a little less true than it used to be in Delaware, but it's still usually the case in Ocean City. Therefore, planning ahead is smart even off-season, though you can probably go on the spur of the moment and manage.

Even trying to be clever, like booking inland 30 to 50 miles, doesn't always work, especially on summer weekends when more than one special event in different beach towns ensures that desirable hotels everywhere on the peninsula are pretty well booked.

Whatever time of year you visit, a highlight of any trip to the shore is the food. The restaurants may change, in some cases from one year to the next, but the cuisine remains focused on seafood, fast food, and comfort food.

With regard to seafood, the region's blue crabs often take precedence in visitors' thoughts, but there's much more. Fresh rockfish is a distinct delicacy, especially when it's truly fresh, like from the previous day's catch.

Fast food is self-explanatory, and many of these restaurants (and stands) can be found on the boardwalks in Ocean City and Rehoboth Beach.

Comfort food is another story, and there are many options for upscale mac and cheese, and the like.

After all, eating is certainly part of the beach experience. A day spent on the water or playing in the sand will have whetted your appetite.

Luckily for you, the locale—so close to waterways and fertile land—offers wonderful fresh food.

IN THE AREA

Bethany Beach, Delaware

Attractions and Recreation

BETHANY BEACH BOOKS. Call 302-539-2522. Website: www.bethany beachbooks.com.

Fenwick Island, Delaware

Attractions and Recreation

FENWICK ISLAND LIGHTHOUSE. Website: fenwickislandlighthouse.org.

Ocean City, Maryland

Attractions and Recreation

BOARDWALK, with arcade games, rides, saltwater taffy, pizza, French fries, and beautiful views of the ocean.

Dining/Drinks

FAGER'S ISLAND RESTAURANT. Call 410-524-5500. Website: fagers.com.

SHARK ON THE HARBOR, West Ocean City. Call 410-213-0924. Website: www.ocshark.com.

SUNSET GRILLE, West Ocean City. Call 410-213-8110. Website: ocsunset grille.com.

THE ANGLER. Call 410-289-7424. Website: www.angleroc.net.

Rehoboth Beach, Delaware

Accommodations

THE BELLMOOR INN & SPA. Call 302-227-5800. Website: www.thebell moor.com.

BOARDWALK PLAZA HOTEL. Call 302-227-7169 or 1-800-332-3224. Website: www.boardwalkplaza.com.

Attractions and Recreation

BROWSEABOUT BOOKS. Call 302-226-2665. Website: www.browseabout books.com.

DELAWARE DIVISION OF FISH & WILDLIFE. Call 302-739-9918. Website: www.fw.delaware.gov.

DELAWARE SURF FISHING. Website: www.delaware-surf-fishing.com.

GORDONS POND TRAIL. Website: www.lewes.com/events-and-activities /biking-a-hiking/62-gordons-pond-trail.html.

JUNCTION AND BREAKWATER TRAIL. Website: www.leweschamber .com/trails/junction-breakwater-biking-and-hiking-trail.

TANGER OUTLETS. Call 302-226-9223 or 1-866-665-8682. Website: www .tangeroutlet.com/rehoboth.

Dining/Drinks

CHESAPEAKE & MAINE. Call 302-226-3600. Website: www.dogfish.com /restaurants/chesapeake-maine.

THE CULTURED PEARL. Call 302-227-8493. Website: www.culturedpearl .us.

Stevensville, Maryland

Attractions and Recreation

CHESAPEAKE BAY BRIDGE TRAFFIC INFO. Website: baybridge.com.

KENT ISLAND EXPRESS, drive-over service for Chesapeake Bay Bridge. Call 410-604-0486. Website: www.kentislandexpress.com.

7

WANDERING BREATHTAKING DU PONT ESTATES

ESTIMATED LENGTH: 220 miles round-trip from Baltimore; 150 miles round-trip from Philadelphia

ESTIMATED TIME: 3–4 days

GETTING THERE: From Baltimore to The Inn at Montchanin Village, take I-95 North toward New York. Take the I-295 exit toward the New Jersey Turnpike and Delaware Memorial Bridge. Merge onto DE 141 North toward Newport for 6.8 miles and turn left onto Montchanin Road (DE 100) for 1.1 miles. The inn is just past Carpenters Row.

HIGHLIGHTS: Over-the-top opulence and grandeur at Winterthur and Nemours, where it all started at the Hagley gunpowder mill, former DuPont workers' homes turned luxury inn at Montchanin Village, DuPont nylon factory exhibit at the Seaford Museum, HOTEL DU PONT, Longwood Gardens.

The Brandywine Valley is frequently referred to as "chateau country," a reference to the natural beauty as well as to the Du Pont family heritage that began in France. We'll start by visiting the Du Pont gardens, mansions, and estates that make up part of the valley in this chapter, then follow it up with art and food venues in the next chapter.

Once you get to the **Wilmington** area, everything in this itinerary is close by. The HOTEL DU PONT and The Playhouse on Rodney Square (formerly the DuPont Theatre) are downtown, not far off DE 52. From downtown Wilmington, you can follow DE 52 North to reach Hagley Museum and Library and then Nemours Mansion and Gardens.

By traveling a few miles farther on DE 52 North, you'll come to Winterthur Museum, Garden & Library. Continuing just over the Pennsylvania

LOBBY OF HOTEL DU PONT

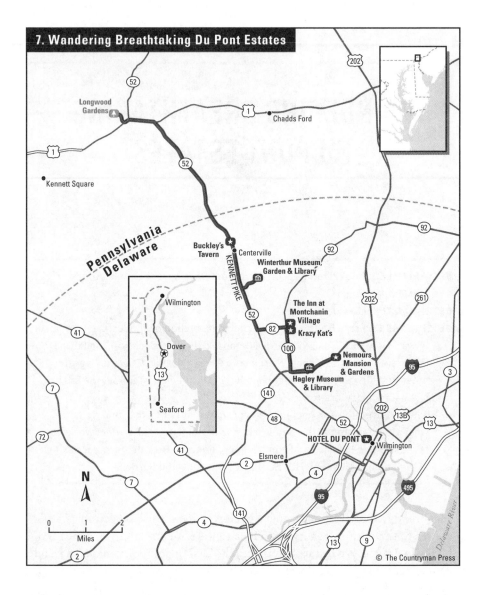

state line on PA 52 to US 1, you'll reach Longwood Gardens. The Inn at Montchanin Village is close to everything also, making it easy to get around to visit the Du Pont estates in whatever order suits you.

The caveat for this trip is that the area is so rich in beauty—both natural and artistic—that you cannot see or absorb everything in one trip. While a lot is contained in this and the next chapter, take it slowly. Such exquisite beauty deserves that you pause to comprehend what you're seeing and stop long enough to appreciate it.

You must believe that you'll come back, and so you don't need to see everything now, for the many charms here are alluring. Also, the gardens vary from season to season, and you'll want to visit them at more than one time of year. There is truly an abundance of riches in the Du Pont legacy. In many ways, it's advisable to pace yourself; otherwise it is simply overwhelming.

After all, you couldn't absorb all the art in the Louvre in one day. The Brandywine Valley is just as rich in its own way.

The Brandywine Valley extends across the Delaware-Pennsylvania border, which is not so surprising because Delaware was part of Pennsylvania during colonial days. Besides, Mother Nature doesn't adhere to political boundaries; it's generally the other way around.

Delaware was originally part of the territory William Penn controlled. It was only on the eve of independence from the British crown that Delaware also asserted its independence from Pennsylvania.

The Du Pont dynasty in America began in 1800, when Pierre-Samuel Du Pont de Nemours and his sons, including Eleuthère Irénée (E.I.), left France and settled on the banks of the Brandywine River. Within two years they had bought land, and within another two years they had built what quickly became a successful gunpowder mill. This led them to amass great wealth and become one of the richest families in the United States. As a result, the Du Ponts left their stamp on the art and architecture of the Brandywine Valley, as well as in many other arenas.

HAGLEY'S FORMER GUNPOWDER OPERATION

The Du Ponts were responsible for providing armaments, specifically gunpowder, to the government in the War of 1812 and to the Union army during the Civil War. They also created nylon, which greatly assisted the Allies in winning World War II, and they even developed the nonstick coating Teflon in 1938.

E. I. Du Pont arrived in this country from France with his father and was responsible for building the family's gunpowder mill on the banks of the Brandywine River. E.I. also built Eleutherian Mills as his home on the hill above the mill, and so began the Du Pont fortune. During the War of 1812, the mill had to expand production to keep up with demand. The original Du Pont Powder Mill, along with Eleutherian Mills, is now the Hagley Museum and Library.

To house some of the mill's laborers, E.I. built several homes in the nearby hamlet of **Montchanin** (which later became part of Henry Francis Du Pont's estate at Winterthur). By 1859, Montchanin had workers' houses, a blacksmith shop, and a small school. In 1889, a permanent railroad station was established in Montchanin to transport the Du Pont gunpowder.

The Du Ponts were as close to nobility as the United States got, and they prospered and lived well. Witnessing the beauty of the art and land they possessed is overwhelming. If you can swing it, you'll want to stay in equally gorgeous properties, in keeping with the nature of this trip.

With that in mind, you will be happy, happy, and happiest if you stay at **The Inn at Montchanin Village**. (The name Montchanin, pronounced *monn-shannon*, with a silent "t," is in honor of Anne Alexandrine de Montchanin, grandmother of E. I. Du Pont.) This charming inn is part of the Du Pont heritage, given that it was originally built to house some of the laborers who worked at the gunpowder mill.

Around the turn of the twenty-first century, the village was restored and converted into an exquisite inn with 28 one-of-a-kind rooms and suites. It's upscale and delightful, and located 5 miles northwest of Wilmington, just south of the Pennsylvania border. From the inn you can easily traverse the domain that once was, and still is, marked by the Du Ponts.

From the moment you arrive, you'll be delighted, for the reception area and gathering room in the restored 1850 barn is as upscale as it gets. The inn generously provides iced and hot tea, biscotti, and as many Hershey's Kisses as you can consume, 24 hours a day, along with an honor bar in the evening.

Whimsical signage—subtle crow and cow artistry—is hidden in each bathroom, often inset into a tile or two.

The inn is a member of Historic Hotels of America and on the National Register of Historic Places. It's in a great location with fertile land that feeds the lovely gardens on the property.

This is the perfect place to stay if you want to tour Winterthur, Longwood Gardens, and Nemours, or if you simply want a lovely romantic retreat and don't plan to leave the property. You can have all your meals here at **Krazy Kat's Restaurant**, even work out in the small fitness room if you want exercise. You can also head to nearby **Buckley's Tavern** in **Centreville** for dinner if you want to go off the property.

It's a good idea to schedule appointments at the spa several weeks in advance; you can always try for last-minute, but to make sure you get the services you want, plan ahead. Dinner reservations can be made a few days in advance.

In the evening, you can wander into the stone barn to enjoy late-night drinks at the honor bar or just read or talk. The barn has a vaulted ceiling, thick wooden beams, and beautiful furnishings. This is Du Pont country after all, and luxury is assumed. You won't be disappointed.

Assuming you can tear yourself away from the inn, a great place to start seeing more of the Du Pont heritage is the **Nemours Mansion and Gardens**. You won't want to leave there either.

Visiting several of the Du Pont mansions and gardens in one long weekend is certainly doable. However, the grandeur, opulence, and sheer size of the estates are best absorbed slowly and appreciatively. One a day is quite enough, especially if you're already planning to return to this entrancing valley.

Assuming you take this approach, Nemours is a good place to start, and it's only 2.5 miles from the inn. This 47,000-square-foot Louis XIV-style chateau has 79 rooms and is built on 300 gorgeous acres. To get there from the inn, take DE 100 South (Montchanin Road). Turn left onto DE 141 North (Barley Mill Road) and then left again onto DE 141 North (New Bridge Road/Powder Mill Road). Take a slight right to 850 Alapocas Drive. It's best to check in advance for tour times and days.

Nemours is not as dramatically opulent and elaborately extensive as the Chateau of Versailles in France, but it is in the same vein and it *is* gorgeous, even over-the-top. This is not surprising, for the estate was patterned after

---

DuPont, Du Pont, or du Pont?

Originally the French surname was du Pont.

There's no specific rhyme or reason to modern-day variations. For instance, the formerly named DuPont Theatre is located in the same complex as HOTEL DU PONT, written in all caps.

There's no consistency, but generally the rule is that when referencing the company you use DuPont and when referencing the family you use Du Pont. Beyond that, the spelling seems to depend upon the person doing the spelling.

SCULPTURE ON THE ESTATE AT NEMOURS

Marie Antoinette's Petit Trianon—her private chateau on the extensive grounds at Versailles.

Alfred I. Du Pont built this modern Versailles for his second wife and named it after Nemours, his family's ancestral home in France.

A visit to Nemours works like this: You start at the visitor center, where there is parking. Then you get on a shuttle bus that takes you to see a set of impressive gates before you tour three floors of the mansion. You are then allowed to wander around the spectacular grounds, with elaborate pools and statuary, on your own. Afterward you get back on the shuttle bus at a designated pickup spot and drive through some of the gardens before heading back to the visitor center.

Priceless works of art are on display throughout the mansion. Visiting it is like being in an art gallery. Alfred loved clocks, so there are many gorgeous timepieces, and each chandelier or clock is more spectacular than the next. There are also 24 fireplaces; 22 bathrooms; a music room with a Steinway piano; and beautiful tulipwood, mahogany, and rosewood throughout.

Quite naturally for an estate of this size, the house contains a nanny's quarters and nursery. Alfred also had a billiards room and a bowling alley built in the home. Outside, the grounds are very Versailles-like, with a large reflecting pool for swimming and boating, sunken gardens, and fabulous statues. The original estate was 3,000 acres; it's now one-tenth of that. That's still plenty big.

The Du Pont family is aristocracy. They came from France and created their dynasty in America. After becoming rich from making armaments, they became art connoisseurs, philanthropists, and collectors. They built schools, hospitals, roads, and a cultural heritage in the Brandywine Valley. In large part as a result of their influence, Delaware (and a small portion of Pennsylvania) is what it is today.

After visiting Nemours, return to Montchanin and enjoy dinner at Krazy Kat's on the inn's grounds. If it's a lovely night, you can sit outside in Adirondack chairs, imagining, for just a moment, that you live here.

In the morning, you can have breakfast while deciding if you want to see more of the Du Ponts' art and architecture. To gain more insight about them from historic tales of their business acumen, a visit to the **Hagley Museum and Library** is in order. After all, that's where it all began. The business side of the Du Pont fortune is just as interesting as the places they built to enjoy that fortune.

Hagley is only 2 miles from the inn. Take DE 100 South (Montchanin Road). Turn left onto DE 141 North (Barley Mill Road) and take the first left onto Old Barley Mill Road. Then turn left onto Hagley Creek Road; Hagley is at 200 Hagley Creek Road.

Hagley is in a bucolic location—235 acres along the Brandywine River. There the Du Pont family made a fortune on gunpowder—kind of an ironic setting for a rather violently used product. Many safeguards were built into the production process, for a spark could cause an explosion and endanger the men who mixed the black powder. The Brandywine River, besides being lovely, was integral to operating the gunpowder mill.

The Du Ponts ended up with hundreds of patents for machinery used in the production process. Later on, these patents would prove valuable in contributing to the family's vast fortune.

Visitors to Hagley can see both the gunpowder mill and the first Du Pont home built in America, Eleutherian Mills, and its garden.

You might also decide to visit **Winterthur Museum, Garden & Library** (pronounced *winter-turr*) on DE 52 between I-95 and US 1. Winterthur was once the home of Henry Francis Du Pont. It's really a mansion, in every sense of the word, on 1,000 acres of gorgeous landscape. At one time, many workers lived on the estate with their families. In addition to the extensive garden, the antiques and architectural details in the museum are amazing.

From the inn, take DE 100 South (Montchanin Road). Take the first right onto State Route 82 and then another right onto DE 52 North (Kennett Pike). Turn right onto Winterthur Road. The museum is at 5105 Kennett Pike.

When you arrive at Winterthur, park your car and enter the visitor center. From there, you can ride a tram through the 60-acre garden. If you have kids along, you can wander in the 3-acre Enchanted Woods children's garden.

Winterthur is a wooded, naturalistic estate, with gates used around the grounds to entice entrance into specific areas.

In addition to a garden tour, a variety of tours are available through some of the 175 rooms in the mansion. Amazingly, more than 50 sets of dishes were used to entertain, and visitors get to see some of them. Visitors also are allowed to wander on their own through the galleries, where a permanent collection and special traveling exhibitions are on display.

Besides the tram, there's a shuttle bus that makes a continuous loop between the museum, the museum store, and the visitor center. Or you can reboard the tram at the museum.

It's all so much. And yet there's still more.

E.I.'s great-grandson Pierre Samuel Du Pont helped create the DuPont corporate empire in the early 20th century. Besides helping to expand the family business in such a dramatic fashion, he also established **Longwood Gardens**. Longwood turned out to be a horticultural marvel, with fountains, meadows, a conservatory, an indoor children's garden, and much more. It is located in Kennett Square, Pennsylvania, not far over the Delaware state line and only about 30 miles west of Philadelphia.

To get to Longwood, follow DE 52 North across the Pennsylvania state line, where it turns slightly left and becomes PA 52 North/US 1 South. Drive less than a mile and take the exit to Country Club Road/Longwood Road. Continue to 1001 Longwood Road.

If you love flowers, a visit to Longwood Gardens is *de rigueur,* or essential.

ON THE GROUNDS AT WINTERTHUR

Be prepared to be overwhelmed. Longwood is a little larger than the 1,000-acre Winterthur and there's even a topiary garden at Longwood, along with just about everything a backyard gardener would envy.

As president of the DuPont Company, Pierre also approved construction of the Hotel du Pont in downtown Wilmington; it was attached to the company's then-corporate headquarters. The hotel opened in 1913 and celebrated its 100th anniversary in 2013. As an alternative to The Inn at Montchanin Village, the now-designated **HOTEL DU PONT** is a grande dame hotel in the European model.

A member of Historic Hotels of America, the hotel is rather self-contained and oh-so-beautiful. Plus, the service is exquisite. There's even a 1,252-seat theater on the premises, **The Playhouse on Rodney Square** (formerly the DuPont Theatre), billed as the country's oldest continuously operating legitimate theater. Many major stars have graced its stage. The **Green Room** is the luxury restaurant within the hotel where hotel guests, local business executives, and city residents frequently dine; it's a beautiful, rather formal room.

If you time it properly when there's a show in town, you can dine *and* go to the theater, all from within the hotel. For a special occasion or just "because," HOTEL DU PONT is about as good as it gets.

Winding up the Du Pont story is not easy, for the family is so prevalent, so dominant in Delaware history. The Du Ponts even spill over into Pennsylvania's share of the Brandywine Valley and into Maryland along the upper Chesapeake Bay.

But there's also the town of **Seaford** in southwestern Delaware, which has a major Du Pont connection.

The DuPont Company was the first and main manufacturer of nylon, and its giant nylon factory was located in Seaford. Situated alongside the **Nanticoke River**, the factory had an easy mode of transport for the factory's goods.

In its heyday, the nylon factory employed nearly half the area's workforce. While you're driving north and south in the state, you'll probably notice that US 13 is also named the DuPont Highway. The Du Ponts built the highway, and it came in handy when the factory in Seaford was built.

The **Seaford Museum** is unusually excellent for a town museum. One of its exhibits is about the nylon factory that in many ways created the town. The factory is gone, but it's obviously well remembered.

To reach the Seaford Museum from Wilmington, travel on US 13 South to the other end of the state. Turn right onto DE 20 West. Then turn left onto North Front Street and right onto High Street. The museum is at the corner of High and Conwell Streets in the old Seaford Post Office building.

Seaford Museum is open Thursday through Sunday afternoons. **Bon Appetit Restaurant** is right on High Street, close to the museum; it's a good choice for lunch or dinner.

IN THE AREA

Seaford

Attractions and Recreation

SEAFORD MUSEUM. Call 302-628-9828. Website: www.seafordhistorical society.com/visit/seaford-museum.

Dining/Drinks

BON APPÉTIT RESTAURANT. Call 302-629-3700. Website: www.bon appetitseaford.com.

Wilmington

Accommodations

HOTEL DU PONT. Call 302-594-3100 or 1-800-441-9019. Website: www .hoteldupont.com.

THE INN AT MONTCHANIN VILLAGE & SPA, Montchanin. Call 302-888-2133 or 1-800-269-2473. Website: www.montchanin.com.

Attractions and Recreation

THE PLAYHOUSE ON RODNEY SQUARE. Call 302-888-0200.

HAGLEY MUSEUM AND LIBRARY. Call 302-658-2400. Website: www .hagley.org.

LONGWOOD GARDENS, Kennett Square, PA. Call 610-388-1000. Website: www.longwoodgardens.org.

NEMOURS MANSION AND GARDENS. Call 302-651-6912 or 1-800-651-6912. Website: nemoursestate.org.

WINTERTHUR MUSEUM, GARDEN & LIBRARY. Call 302-888-4600 or 1-800-448-3883. Website: www.winterthur.org.

Dining/Drinks

BUCKLEY'S TAVERN, Centreville. Call 302-656-9776. Website: www
.buckleystavern.com.

GREEN ROOM, in HOTEL DU PONT. Call 302-594-3154. Website: www
.hoteldupont.com/green-room-en.html.

KRAZY KAT'S RESTAURANT, at the Inn at Montchanin Village. Call 302-
888-4200. Website: www.krazykatsrestaurant.net.

WEST CHESTER

LITTLE FREE LIBRARY

Take One or Leave One

8

EXPLORING THE BRANDYWINE VALLEY'S RICHES

ESTIMATED LENGTH: 200 miles round-trip from Baltimore

ESTIMATED TIME: 3 days

GETTING THERE: Take DE 52 North from Wilmington or I-95 South from Philadelphia to DE 52 North. From DE 52 North, turn right onto US 1 North. The Brandywine River Museum will be about 3.5 miles on the right, just before Creek Road. Alternatively, you can drive from the Baltimore Beltway onto US 1 North across the Conowingo Dam and farmland into Pennsylvania until you reach the museum in Chadds Ford.

HIGHLIGHTS: Chadds Ford, West Chester, Brandywine River Museum of Art, Baldwin's Book Barn, Kennett Square (Mushroom Capital of the World), Longwood Gardens.

This itinerary is a journey in threes: mushrooms, a bookstore, and art—a fabulous combination—and Chadds Ford, West Chester, and Kennett Square—three appealing little towns.

The Brandywine Valley straddles the Delaware-Pennsylvania border. For this trip, you'll visit three towns related in part to the Du Ponts but also vital to the agricultural and cultural importance of an area less than an hour from Philadelphia but light-years from the urban scene.

Everyone seems to be on a first-name basis with their neighbors, the beauty of the rich valley is captured in significant art, the mushrooms are world-class, and the food is both sophisticated and gourmet. However, the pace is slow, relaxed, and deliberate.

This is the perfect place to spend an afternoon or an overnight. There are a few hotels as well as several charming bed-and-breakfasts.

WEST CHESTER LITTLE FREE LIBRARY

To see how the Wyeths and other artists captured the natural beauty of the landscape and the people of the valley, take US 1 to the **Brandywine River Museum of Art** in **Chadds Ford**.

But first, if you're hungry, stop for breakfast or lunch at **Hank's Place**, which is across from the museum at the junction of US 1 and Creek Road. Hank's is an excellent local diner where artist Andrew Wyeth was known to dine frequently.

At Hank's, consider ordering a mushroom omelet. Prepare to be delighted, for it's sure to be made with delicious fresh local mushrooms. Chadds Ford is near the village of Kennett Square, which is known as the Mushroom Capital of the World. You'll visit Kennett Square later in this trip, but for now, settle for ordering a dish made with local mushrooms.

The little town of Chadds Ford is built along the banks of the Brandywine River. That's where you'll find the charming Brandywine River Museum of Art in a former 19th-century gristmill with original structural beams, white plaster walls, and pine floors, along with many modern touches. The

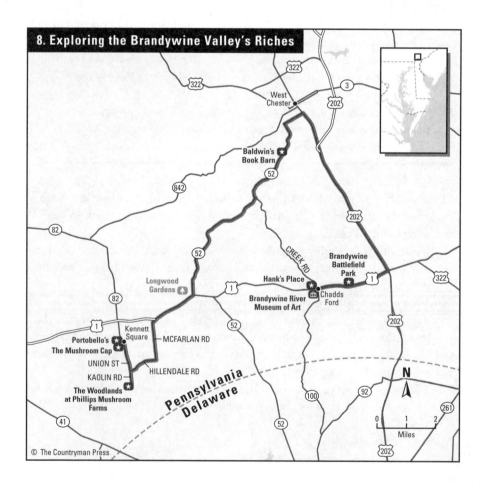

8. Exploring the Brandywine Valley's Riches

© The Countryman Press

ANDREW WYETH'S STUDIO AT BRANDYWINE RIVER MUSEUM OF ART

museum is tucked into nature, fitting in well with the charm of the river outside its walls and the surrounding trees and vegetation.

This world-class art museum is famous for its collection of Wyeths. One
of the most popular artists from these parts is Andrew Wyeth, known for
melancholy sentimental landscapes. His father, N. C. Wyeth, was a successful and witty book illustrator, and his son Jamie Wyeth is known for several famous portraits. Spend an hour or two at the museum reveling in the
beauty of the American art displayed there.

During part of the year (April through November), visitors can tour the
studio where Andrew Wyeth worked to get a sense of his life as an artist
in such a rustic setting. There's a separate charge for the studio tour, and
advance reservations are sometimes required. You reach the studio via a
jitney (a small bus) taken from the museum.

A separate tour of the N. C. Wyeth House and Studio, as well as a tour
of the Kuerner Farm, which inspired Andrew Wyeth's artistic imagination,
are handled the same way. If you'd prefer not to plan in advance by making
reservations, there is plenty to see in the museum without taking any of
the tours.

Besides the permanent exhibitions, where the artwork is rotated, the
museum also has regularly scheduled special exhibitions, which are

CONOWINGO DAM ACROSS THE SUSQUEHANNA RIVER, ALONG ONE ROUTE FROM BALTIMORE TO BRANDYWINE VALLEY

well-conceived and well-presented. There's also a lovely gift shop on-site and a small, cheerful restaurant where you serve yourself cafeteria-style.

If you're a history buff, keep in mind the **Brandywine Battlefield Park** in Chadds Ford. During the Revolutionary War, the important Battle of Brandywine, which the Americans lost, was fought here. This loss forced George Washington and his troops to withdraw to Philadelphia. Luckily, the Americans lost the battle but not the war.

After you leave Chadds Ford, take US 1 North a little more than a mile and turn left onto US 202 North/US 322 West. Continue about 6 miles into the village of **West Chester** to do a little shopping and have dinner at one of the excellent restaurants there, including **Limoncello Ristorante** and the **Iron Hill Brewery & Restaurant**. When shopping, make sure to visit **The 5 Senses**, a small boutique gift shop filled with *objets de désir* (desirable objects) made by local artisans.

West Chester is filled with quirky things, like the West Chester Little Free Library—a wooden box of sorts mounted alongside the street with about 50 books inside and a sign that says take one or leave one.

Then there's the town drinking fountain. Dating to 1869, it was designed for use by people, horses, and dogs. In 1987, the fountain was restored to its original site in front of the courthouse, where it stands today—a curiosity.

There are several bed-and-breakfasts in the area. **Faunbrook Bed &**

Breakfast, in particular, is excellent. The house and grounds are impressive, the location is convenient, and the hosts are very accommodating. Most B&Bs profess to make adjustments for guests' dietary preferences at breakfast, but not all mean it. At Faunbrook, the hosts make sure breakfast meets your needs, and they do so pleasantly.

The town of West Chester is also home to the lovely **Baldwin's Book Barn**. Baldwin's enormous five-story stone barn was constructed by Quakers in 1822 and functioned as a dairy barn until the Great Depression. In 1946, right after the end of World War II, William and Lilla Baldwin bought the barn. They moved their used books and collectibles business from Wilmington, Delaware, where they had started it in 1934, into the converted barn in West Chester. The book barn is only about 2 miles outside downtown West Chester. To get there, take PA 52 South (Lenape Road); the barn is at 865 Lenape Road.

Baldwin's has an antique potbellied stove, worn wooden floors and beams, several cats wandering around, numerous cozy nooks, and lovely arched doorways. The store stocks about 250,000 books, some more used than others. There are first editions and others less valuable. For those who love books, or if books are one of your weaknesses, this is a place you shouldn't miss. Baldwin's also carries old manuscripts, maps, and other collectibles.

DOORWAY AT BALDWIN'S BOOK BARN LEADING TO MANY TREASURES

MUSHROOM FARM IN KENNETT SQUARE

Book lovers could spend hours at Baldwin's. The shop has something for everyone, from 25-cent paperbacks to expensive rare editions.

Old books at Baldwin's are not the only old things around. West Chester is also known for its ghosts. There's one tale of a horse thief who was placed in a pillory and punished with lashes. His moans and cries are reportedly still heard today.

Besides offering a lot of books, West Chester is a great place to enjoy excellent meals. It's also a college town, with West Chester University, the county seat, and the headquarters of shopping giant QVC.

Anatomy of a Mushroom

A mushroom is an unusual vegetable, and it's also a fungus grown in dark, moist conditions. The growers of the Brandywine Valley, like those elsewhere in the world, have embraced the science that quantifies growth cycles and agricultural techniques.

Mushrooms come in many types, shapes, and sizes, including white, crimini, shiitake, oyster, maitake, portobello, enoki, pom pom, and chanterelle, among many others.

In ancient Egypt, the pharaohs believed that mushrooms, which appeared mysteriously, were divine and magical, perhaps created by lightning bolts from heaven. This legend was adopted into Greek mythology, and in later Roman times, mushrooms were made part of the Mediterranean cuisine.

Before you leave the area, make sure to visit the small town of **Kennett Square**, which is recognized as the Mushroom Capital of the World. The town produces somewhere in the neighborhood of 500 to 600 million pounds of mushrooms annually, amounting to about 65 percent of the entire US mushroom production. Kennett Square mushrooms are absolutely delicious, from basic white and brown button caps to specialty varieties.

You can buy mushrooms to take home or order a dish made with mushrooms at one of the local restaurants. Either way, they're a treat.

The mushroom farms are rarely open for tours, with one or two exceptions. During the annual **Mushroom Festival**, which takes place the first weekend after Labor Day each year, a few farms usually allow people to glimpse the breeding, growth, and harvesting of these edible fungi.

Phillips is one of the largest mushroom farm complexes in Kennett Square. There is a stone house on the property, **The Woodlands at Phillips Mushroom Farms**, that is the original family home dating to 1828. The house is now a store where the Phillips farm sells mushrooms in season and mushroom-related products such as marinated and dried mushrooms, as well as cookbooks, knickknacks, and souvenirs like metal key chains that say "mushroom" on them.

To get there from West Chester, take PA 52 South (Lenape Road) to US 1 South. Turn left onto McFarlan Road, followed by a right onto East Hillendale Road and a left onto Kaolin Road. The Woodlands at Phillips is at 1020 Kaolin Road.

In town, there's a shop-museum combination called **The Mushroom Cap**. To reach town, drive north on Kaolin Road, which becomes South Union Street. Follow that about 1 mile, then turn left onto West State Street. The Mushroom Cap is at 114 West State Street. On the next block at 108 East State Street is **Portabellos**, where you can dine on exquisite mushroom soup, mushrooms and pasta, and just about anything with mushrooms. The mushrooms are ultra fresh, and the chef is brilliant.

In addition to mushrooms, Kennett Square is the location of the Du Ponts' **Longwood Gardens**—a gardener's and horticulturist's dream. The plants in bloom vary depending on the season, but Longwood is invariably delightful.

IN THE AREA

Chadds Ford

Attractions and Recreation

BRANDYWINE BATTLEFIELD PARK. Call 610-459-3342. Website: brandywinebattlefield.org.

BRANDYWINE RIVER MUSEUM OF ART. Call 610-388-2700. Website: www.brandywinemuseum.org.

Dining/Drinks

HANK'S PLACE. Call 610-388-7061. Website: hanksplacechaddsford.com.

Kennett Square

Attractions and Recreation

MUSHROOM FESTIVAL, held in September. Call 610-925-3373 or 1-888-440-9920. Website: www.mushroomfestival.org.

LONGWOOD GARDENS. Call 610-388-1000. Website: www.longwood gardens.org.

THE MUSHROOM CAP. Call 610-444-8484 or 1-866-924-8484. Website: www.themushroomcap.com.

THE WOODLANDS AT PHILLIPS MUSHROOM FARMS. Call 610-444-2192. Wesbite: www.thewoodlandsatphillips.com.

Dining/Drinks

PORTABELLOS. Call 610-925-4984. Website: www.portabellosofkennett square.com.

West Chester

Accommodations

FAUNBROOK BED & BREAKFAST. Call 610-436-5788. Website: www.faun brook.com.

Attractions and Recreation

BALDWIN'S BOOK BARN. Call 610-696-0816. Website: www.bookbarn .com.

THE 5 SENSES. Call 610-719-0170. Website: www.the5senses.com.

Dining/Drinks

IRON HILL BREWERY & RESTAURANT. Call 610-738-9600. Website: www .ironhillbrewery.com.

LIMONCELLO RISTORANTE. Call 610-436-6230. Website: limoncello restaurant.com.

9

TAKING THE FERRY FROM LEWES TO CAPE MAY AND BACK AGAIN

ESTIMATED LENGTH: 280 miles round-trip plus about 30 nautical miles back and forth on the ferry across the Delaware Bay

ESTIMATED TIME: 3–4 days

GETTING THERE: From Philadelphia and Wilmington, take I-95 South to DE 1 South. Follow DE 1 South for 92 miles. Turn left to go east on DE 9 Business Route (Savannah Road) toward Lewes. Follow DE 9 Business Route 2.5 miles into Lewes.

From the Chesapeake Bay Bridge, follow US 50 East. Turn left onto MD 404 East, which becomes DE 404 East in Delaware. In Georgetown, go three-quarters of the way around the roundabout and continue on DE 9 East to Lewes.

HIGHLIGHTS: Cape May–Lewes Ferry, town of Lewes with boutique shops and War of 1812 history, town of Cape May, dolphins, whale watching, Cape May diamonds, superb restaurants, Cape May Lighthouse, Sunset Beach, World War II fortifications at Cape Henlopen and Cape May.

In this itinerary, you have options, which is always great. A trip between the "Twin Capes"—**Cape May**, New Jersey, and **Cape Henlopen**, Delaware (just outside **Lewes**)—can be done by car the long way around or by ferry, either with your car or on foot. For our purposes here, let's assume you'll be traveling with your car on the ferry.

First, focus on the definition of a cape, which is a curved peninsula, usually formed where competing currents push the sand around. On these two capes, located on either side of the Delaware Bay where it meets the Atlantic

CAPE MAY LIGHTHOUSE

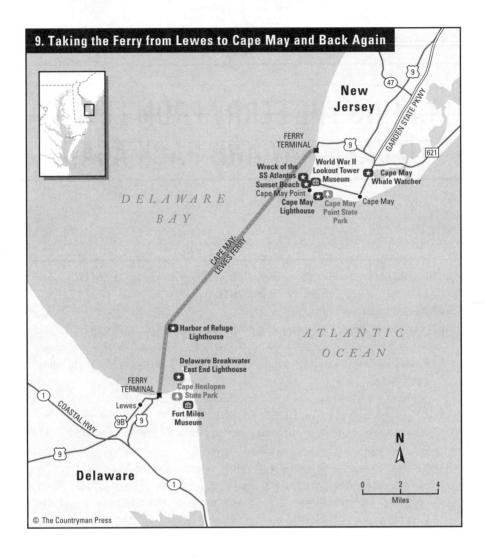

New Jersey

GARDEN STATE PKWY

47

9

621

FERRY TERMINAL

9

Wreck of the SS Atlantus

Sunset Beach

Cape May Point

World War II Lookout Tower Museum

Cape May Whale Watcher

Cape May Lighthouse

Cape May Point State Park

Cape May

D E L A W A R E

B A Y

CAPE MAY–LEWES FERRY

Harbor of Refuge Lighthouse

A T L A N T I C

O C E A N

Delaware Breakwater East End Lighthouse

Cape Henlopen State Park

FERRY TERMINAL

1

COASTAL HWY

Lewes

9B 9

Fort Miles Museum

9

1

Delaware

N

0 2 4
Miles

© The Countryman Press

Ocean, currents from the ocean intermingle with those from the bay. Thus, the two capes are formed and maintained.

Whether you start out in Lewes or reverse the trip and begin in Cape May, the first stop is the ferry terminal, where you will wait in line before driving your car onto the ferry, parking, and wandering around on board. The ferry provides restrooms, fast food, tables and chairs, and several decks from which you can watch the scenery. It's your choice whether to stay inside or outside, or mix it up.

Lewes, Delaware. The town of Lewes (pronounced *lew-is* or *loo-iss,* after the town of the same name in East Sussex, England) is a charming, historic, upscale place that will make you smile as you stop in somewhere for coffee or ice cream, buy a present for yourself or someone back home, browse at **Biblion Used Books & Rare Finds,** and take the ferry over to the New Jersey shore for a visit to Cape May.

Your best bet is to stay at **The Inn at Canal Square,** a charming inn with 22 rooms and 3 suites. The rooms are delightful, many with views of the canal that extends from Lewes to Rehoboth Beach, and the service is attentive and friendly. An excellent European breakfast is included in the nightly charge.

For such a small town, there are superb restaurant options: **Agave Mexican Restaurant & Tequila Bar** if there's not too long a wait, **Half Full** for gourmet pizza and wine, **Rose & Crown** for general all-around good food, and **Striper Bites Bistro** for seafood.

If you want a bit of nightlife, the bar at **Gilligan's Restaurant & Bar,** right outside the door to the inn, is friendly and filled with locals, which always bodes well.

There's a popular ice cream shop, **King's Homemade Ice Cream,** that often looks really crowded, but the line moves quickly.

Lewes is a quiet, rather atypical beach town with high-end boutiques and restaurants that are more upscale than those in the usual beach town. Kids ride their bikes around town, and there's no boardwalk. It's just a small town that is lucky to have beautiful beaches, both in Lewes itself and at the adjacent **Cape Henlopen State Park**.

Cape May, New Jersey. Cape May is a family beach town. There's no longer a boardwalk, not since the nor'easter of 1962. It was replaced with a concrete promenade and seawall, which better protect the town from storms and resulting floods. There's also the pedestrian **Washington Street Mall**. The promenade and mall substitute for a boardwalk, with the requisite T-shirts, fudge, jewelry, and other typical beach items.

Water activities, as in most coastal towns, are prevalent. There's the ferry to and from Lewes, which is perhaps the best deal going. In 85 minutes, the trip encompasses lighthouses, likely dolphin sightings (if you pay attention), snacks, and a fun ride, especially in good weather.

Founded in 1620, Cape May is the oldest seaside city in the United States. Its heyday was perhaps the Victorian era. In the 1970s, many of the gorgeous old Victorian houses were converted into bed-and-breakfasts.

Many of these houses have lovely porches, usually with rocking chairs, as the Victorian lifestyle included sitting on the porch. It's curious to see teenagers today sitting on these porches while focused on their smartphones instead of talking to one another—like a bit of one century mixed with a bit of another, the old mixed with the new.

Originally visitors came to Cape May by steamboat from New York,

Philadelphia, Baltimore, and Virginia. This mode of transport was popular in the 1800s until it was slowly and then more actively replaced by railroad lines. Whatever their method of getting here, city dwellers found the draw of ocean breezes irresistible in pre-air-conditioning days.

A devastating fire in 1878, which wiped out 30 blocks and 35 acres of the seaside resort, created a need for new housing. The fire was in the west end of town. Fire trucks from Camden, 90 miles away, were put on trains to fight the blaze. After the fire, smaller hotels were built, along with a massive number of Victorian-style mansions with gingerbread details.

Looking at Victorian houses in Cape May is nearly impossible to avoid. These beautiful "painted ladies" are located all over town, including on Ocean, Washington, Columbia, Gurney, and Hughes Streets, as well as on Beach, Trenton, and New Jersey Avenues.

Dolphin and whale watching. You obviously need to be out on the water to see dolphins and whales, but bottlenose dolphins often make themselves known to travelers on the ferry across the bay. You can also take a whale and dolphin tour of the Atlantic waters off Cape May through **Cape May Whale Watcher** and see more of the appealing mammals.

Dolphins are fast-moving, generally traveling in pods of 4 to 12, though you can sometimes spot as many as 50 or 60 together in the bay or ocean. Humpback whales are more likely to be seen out in the ocean, especially if they breach, or jump out of the water with a large splash. It's not unusual to see just one whale or perhaps two or three.

On the Cape May–Lewes Ferry, the captain will slow down if a whale is sighted, but he won't reduce speed for dolphins, as they move quickly.

Cape May–Lewes Ferry. The ferry traverses 17 miles (the equivalent of about 14.5 nautical miles) and takes about 85 minutes to cross Delaware Bay between Lewes and Cape May. The ferry doesn't go out into the Atlantic, but instead stays on the bay side of the two capes, just skirting the ocean.

Nautical Terminology

Ebb tide = outgoing tide, out of the bay and up the Atlantic coast
Flood tide = incoming tide, down the beach
Knot = 1.15 miles per hour
Nautical mile = 6,076 feet
Port = left-hand side (facing forward)
Starboard = right-hand side (facing forward)
Statute (regular) mile = 5,280 feet

FERRY PULLING INTO LEWES TERMINAL AT SUNSET

The ferry ride is delightful, so relax and enjoy it. If you're lucky, you'll have glorious weather; most of the passengers will be out on the decks looking at the birds trailing the ship and diving for fish, hoping for dolphin sightings, viewing the lighthouses, and watching other boats go by.

If the weather is inclement, the ferry still travels (unless conditions are really bad). In poor weather, travelers stay inside, eating snacks from the cafeteria, playing cards, napping, reading, and working on laptops.

The ferry runs year-round with one caveat: If the weather is too windy, which can happen even on a Memorial Day weekend, or there are dangerous ice floes in the bay, the trips may be canceled.

An individual ferry may also be delayed if there's a mechanical or personnel issue. The trips need a certain number of crew members and a ship in good working order.

From the ferry, you can see three lighthouses—two on the Delaware side (**Harbor of Refuge Lighthouse** and **Delaware Breakwater East End Lighthouse**) and one in New Jersey (**Cape May Lighthouse**), though the ferry route does not get too close to any of them.

Wildlife is definitely part of the experience. If you're lucky and watch closely when you get between the buoys, and if the water is warm enough, you'll see dolphins. And if you're really lucky, you might see a few whales breach.

Of course, there are always seagulls flying around. And when the propellers kick up at the back of the ferry, they may stir up a herring run, thus attracting gannets, which often fly behind the ship looking for herring. These pointy-beaked birds can dive 5 to 6 feet underwater to get the herring; this is quite a sight.

Flip-flops or sandals are probably all the covering you'll need on your feet in warm weather near the water. However, when you're on the ferry and other boats, you'll want to wear closed shoes with nonskid bottoms for traction.

Even in calm weather, the movement of the ship can cause you to feel wobbly. One ferry captain explained that having "sea legs" means anticipating which way the ship will move next so you're prepared. If you feel woozy on board, the expression "like a drunken sailor" may resonate.

An unusual beach. Seashells and driftwood aside, at **Sunset Beach**, located on the outskirts of Cape May on Delaware Bay, Cape May diamonds are scattered all over the sand and are ripe for the picking.

Unlike sea glass, which is gradually becoming scarce because fewer bottles are made of glass and thus there's less waste from them in the oceans, beach diamonds (called Cape May diamonds in New Jersey and Delaware diamonds in Delaware) are in abundance. They are not really diamonds, of course, but are actually pure quartz crystals. They start out 200 miles north of Cape May, on the upper Delaware River, and land, perhaps thousands of years later, on the beach, where they are collected by enthusiasts.

These "diamonds" look like little frosted pebbles, but they can be tumbled

SUNSET BEACH, WITH REMNANTS OF THE CONCRETE SHIP SS *ATLANTUS* OFFSHORE

for three weeks and made to look clear. Another step, actually polishing and faceting the stones, can make them into diamond look-alikes with some luster and sparkle, as well as a much lower price tag than the real thing.

The area outside Cape May where Sunset Beach is located is considered **Cape May Point**, the former tribal headquarters for the Kechemeche Indians. The Kechemeches were related to Indians in the Algonquin Nation, which included the Nanticokes and Choptanks, among others throughout the Delmarva Peninsula.

The Kechemeches were the first to find Cape May diamonds, and they gave them as gifts to other Indians and later to white settlers. The Indians believed the translucent gems carried mystical powers and brought good fortune.

Visitors to Sunset Beach, at the foot of Sunset Boulevard on Cape May Point, can find the raw stones or buy tumbled and even faceted ones inside the gift shop there, **Sunset Beach Gifts**. There's also a grill for light meals and a mini-golf course. Just don't expect to go swimming; there are no lifeguards on this beach, so swimming is off-limits. If you have the appropriate fishing license, though, you can fish from Sunset Beach. (And you can swim at the beaches in Cape May itself, just not at this one.)

Don't be startled by a large object out in the water off Sunset Beach. That's the **SS *Atlantus***, the relic of a concrete ship built during World War I. A shortage of steel caused the US government to experiment with this unconventional shipbuilding material. Only 12 concrete ships were actually built as part of the World War I fleet, though the United States did build more concrete ships during World War II.

Atlantus was commissioned in 1919–20 to be used as a government-owned commercial coal steamer in New England. It was towed to Cape May in 1926 to be the base of a drawbridge for a prospective ferry service. A series of mishaps, including a major storm in June 1926, left *Atlantus* on Cape May Point. Erosion has put it 200 to 300 feet offshore, where it's an anomaly and a rather absurd attraction.

Sunset Beach got its name due to its location, which has an unobstructed view of the horizon; thus, the sunsets are beautiful. As a special treat from Memorial Day through the end of August, and on Saturdays in September, there's a flag-lowering ceremony on the beach every night at sunset.

Because the shore has eroded over time, in addition to Cape May diamonds, visitors can sometimes find Indian arrowheads and fossil sharks' teeth. Strong outgoing and incoming tides flow against the remnants of *Atlantus*, which propel the diamonds and other items to wash up on the beach. The largest stones are generally found in the wintertime when surf is strong, and especially during storms, though most people come looking for the diamonds in warm weather from spring through fall.

Everyone in town will tell you it's easy to reach Cape May Point and

VIEW FROM THE CAPE MAY LIGHTHOUSE

Sunset Beach. You'll hear more than once that it's straight going, about a mile and a half, and you cannot get lost—you'll just end up in the water. They'll tell you, "Just park before getting wet."

It's fun and tranquil at Sunset Beach, just you, some fishermen, and a scattering of other people looking for diamonds too. Legend has it that Captain Kidd buried his treasure at Sunset Beach, so if you see something gold and shiny, take a good look.

Birding and touring. Outside of town is a quiet, peaceful wildlife and nature refuge. Horseshoe crabs lay eggs on the sand, and birds come and eat them. When this occurs, the beach is roped off, but birders are ever-watchful.

Cape May is on the Atlantic Flyway and is thus a birder's dream. People come from all over the world to watch the birds. For those who love to birdwatch, or those with just a passing interest, it is fascinating.

During heavy migrations in the spring and fall, park rangers are on hand near the Cape May Lighthouse at **Cape May Point State Park** to point out migrating hawks to visitors.

Climbing up into the lighthouse is worthwhile, for there are wonderful 360-degree views at the top. It has a 199-step cast-iron spiral staircase with a landing every 31 steps where you can take breaks from the climb to catch your breath.

The lighthouse was built in 1859. There's also a small museum on the grounds with local history exhibits. The State of New Jersey owns the lighthouse, and the US Coast Guard continues to operate the beacon on top to assist in maritime navigation. The lighthouse reportedly has a few ghosts too.

If lighthouses are your thing, check out the **Delaware Bay Lighthouse Cruise Adventure** as well; it's a cruise to visit the lights of the Delaware Bay visible from the water. This tour is run only a few days during the summer and fall from Cape May.

Other entities running lighthouse tours on Delaware Bay include **Delaware River & Bay Lighthouse Foundation**, with occasional tours and sunset cruises from Lewes. **Cape Water Tours & Taxis** also offers tours during the summer out of Lewes.

There are historic trolley tours in Cape May too, but you can best appreciate the Victorian architecture by driving or walking around the historic district at your own pace. As you turn a corner or walk down a street, you'll be struck by the beauty and grandeur of the restored Victorians. You can walk to several excellent restaurants too, including **Ristorante A Ca Mia** at the Washington Street Mall and the **Washington Inn**.

If you're going to one of the Cape May city beaches from Memorial Day to Labor Day, you'll need to buy a beach tag for everyone in your group who is 12 years or older. There are bike rentals in season, and you can generally ride on the ocean promenade from 6 to 10 a.m. May through October.

One quirk about Cape May is the gasoline pumping law, for it's illegal to pump your own gas in New Jersey. You have to sit and wait for someone who works at the gas station to do it for you—a blast from the past to visitors from other places.

World War II fortifications. Those of us born long after the end of World War II grew up thinking the theaters of war included Europe, North Africa, and the Pacific. We didn't learn much about the dangers to the East Coast of the United States or the fact that the waters off our shores were hazardous.

During the war, Nazi submarines, or U-boats, patrolled the East Coast, torpedoing military and merchant vessels at any opportunity. Sonar and depth charges were used to track down and destroy the U-boats.

Fear was also rampant that German battleships might appear. To protect against the Germans, and to act as a deterrent, **Fort Miles** was built.

Not a fort in the traditional sense, Fort Miles was a series of fire control towers, gun batteries, barracks, and support buildings constructed on both sides of Delaware Bay. The idea was for the coverage areas to overlap. The largest guns were set up on the Delaware side, where Cape Henlopen State Park is now situated, given that the shipping channel hugs the Delaware shore.

Fort Miles was the largest East Coast military installation during World War II. Its presence revived the town of Lewes, where there was a large nightclub, a pool hall, and an alleged brothel, among other businesses that flourished during wartime.

NONDESCRIPT ENTRANCE TO A WORLD WAR II BATTERY AT CAPE HENLOPEN

Luckily, a land invasion never materialized. However, ships did go down in the Atlantic, and Americans were fearful throughout the war.

Cape May's Fire Control Tower No. 23 has been preserved as the **World War II Lookout Tower Museum**, and visitors can climb the restored coastal artillery lookout tower. Once part of the immense harbor defense at Fort Miles, the tower was built in 1942 as one of 15 towers in the system. Inside, a spiral staircase leads to the top.

On the other side of the bay, at former Battery 519 in Cape Henlopen State Park outside Lewes, is the **Fort Miles Museum**. Besides the museum and remnants of Fort Miles's towers and bunkers, the state park there offers beaches, two lighthouses in the harbor, a bird habitat, and gorgeous dunes. It can be moody and somewhat deserted at times, depending on the season and the weather, but it is nonetheless appealing. Calm now reigns on both sides of the Delaware Bay after the serious military threats of World War II. Only remnants, and many memories, survive from that time.

On your way out of Cape May, leave via Washington Street. After the road curves to the left, make a right onto the little bridge at the marina. Follow that street around until you see signs for US 9 South (Sandman Boulevard). Follow the signs to the **Cape May–Lewes Ferry**. When you get to Ferry Road, turn left and stop at the check-in booth.

The only tricky part is the jughandle, where you'll go to the right and partially around in order to go left. *Jughandle* is a New Jersey term for heading to the right in order to come around to the left.

IN THE AREA

Cape May, New Jersey

Accommodations

BED-AND-BREAKFASTS (LIST OF OPTIONS). Website: www.capemay times.com/bed-and-breakfast/cape-may.htm.

Attractions and Recreation

CAPE MAY POINT STATE PARK. Website: www.state.nj.us/dep/parksand forests/parks/capemay.html.

CAPE MAY WHALE WATCHER. Call 609-884-5445 or 1-800-786-5445. Website: www.capemaywhalewatcher.com.

CAPE MAY–LEWES FERRY. Call 1-800-643-3779. Website: www.cmlf.com. Bring a photo ID.

CAPE MAY LIGHTHOUSE. Call 609-884-5404. Website: www.capemaymac .org/cape-may-lighthouse.

DELAWARE BAY LIGHTHOUSE CRUISE ADVENTURE. Call 1-800-275-4278. Webiste: capemaywhalewatcher.com/grand-lighthouse-cruise.php.

SS *ATLANTUS*, in Delaware Bay off Sunset Beach.

SUNSET BEACH GIFTS, plus mini-golf. Call 1-800-757-6468. Website: www .sunsetbeachnj.com.

TROLLEY TOURS (RUN BY MID-ATLANTIC CENTER FOR THE ARTS & HUMANITIES), in and around Cape May. Call 609-884-5404. Website: www.capemaymac.org/trolley-tours.

WASHINGTON STREET MALL. Website: www.heartofcapemay.com.

WORLD WAR II LOOKOUT TOWER MUSEUM. Call 609-884-5064. Website: www.capemaymac.org/world-war-ii-lookout-tower.

Dining/Drinks

RISTORANTE A CA MIA. Call 609-884-6661. Website: www.acamianj.com.

WASHINGTON INN. Call 609-884-5697. Website: www.washingtoninn.com.

Lewes, Delaware

Accommodations

THE INN AT CANAL SQUARE. Call 302-644-3377 or 1-888-644-1911. Website: www.theinnatcanalsquare.com.

Attractions and Recreation

BIBLION USED BOOKS & RARE FINDS. Call 302-644-2210. Website: www.BiblionBooks.com.

CAPE HENLOPEN STATE PARK. Call 302-645-8983. Website: destateparks.com/Beaches/CapeHenlopen.

CAPE MAY–LEWES FERRY. Call 1-800-643-3779. Website: www.cmlf.com. Bring a photo ID.

CAPE WATER TOURS & TAXIS. Call 302-644-7334. Website: www.capewatertaxi.com.

DELAWARE RIVER & BAY LIGHTHOUSE FOUNDATION. Call 302-644-7046. Website: www.delawarebaylights.org.

FORT MILES MUSEUM, Cape Henlopen Park. Call 302-644-5007. Website: destateparks.com/History/FortMiles.

HARBOR OF REFUGE LIGHTHOUSE AND DELAWARE BREAKWATER EAST END LIGHTHOUSE.

Dining/Drinks

AGAVE MEXICAN RESTAURANT & TEQUILA BAR. Call 302-645-1232. Website: agavelewes.com.

GILLIGAN'S RESTAURANT & BAR. Call 302-644-7230. Website: www .gilliganslewes.com.

HALF FULL. Call 302-645-8877. Website: www.halffulllewes.com.

KING'S HOMEMADE ICE CREAM. Call 302-645-9425. Website: www .kingshomemadeicecream.com.

ROSE & CROWN, in Hotel Rodney. Call 302-827-4475. Website: www.rose andcrownlewes.com.

STRIPER BITES BISTRO. Call 302-645-4657. Website: www.striperbites .com.

10

TRACING THE PATH OF THE NANTICOKE AND CHOPTANK INDIANS

ESTIMATED LENGTH: 300 miles round-trip

ESTIMATED TIME: 3–4 days

GETTING THERE: From Baltimore or Washington, DC, take US 50 East outside Annapolis and cross the Chesapeake Bay Bridge (officially the **William Preston Lane, Jr. Memorial Bridge**). Stay on US 50 East, taking the slight right (onto Ocean Gateway/US 50) when the road splits between US 301 North and 50.

> To get to Cambridge, go past Easton and across the Choptank River Bridge. Immediately after crossing the bridge, turn right onto Maryland Avenue and follow the signs to the **Sailwinds Visitor Center**. With its gorgeous views and playground, this is a good place to stretch and let the kids play after being in the car awhile.

HIGHLIGHTS: The Great Mound, Nanticoke Indian Museum, fabulous sunsets at Matapeake Fishing Pier on Kent Island, Native American heritage around rivers and the Chesapeake Bay, Indian trails.

If you're taking this trip in the summertime, note the tall corn, often as high as 6 to 9 feet, growing beside the road. You might even buy some at a roadside stand on your way home. The Indians introduced European settlers to corn, or maize as it's called in Spanish-speaking countries, so this major crop is a testament to their heritage.

While the sweet Maryland corn we eat today is likely a different variety than what the Indians of this region ate, if not for Native Americans, we wouldn't have corn. Indians also used corn husks to weave into moccasins, sleeping mats, and baskets. Corncobs were used for fuel.

REPLICATED INDIAN HOME AT ADKINS ARBORETUM

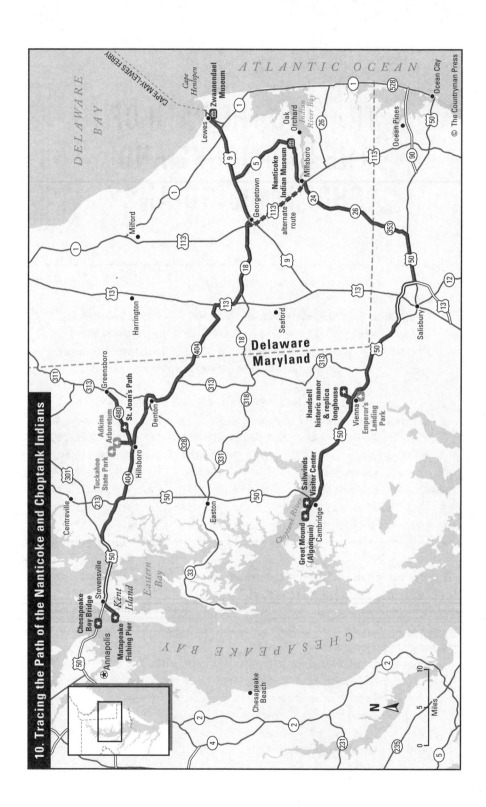

We also find corn useful in many ways. In addition to eating fresh ears of corn, we use the crop to feed chickens and in corn syrup to sweeten many soft drinks. We cook with corn oil and use ethanol made from corn to help fuel our cars.

The growing season for corn in Maryland is generally late June to early October.

Native Americans were living around the Chesapeake Bay and on the Delmarva Peninsula long before European settlers. However, in many ways, their culture is gone, with some exceptions: still remaining are many of their

Indian Names and Words

Chesapeake is actually an Algonquian word meaning "great shellfish bay." The Europeans identified Native Americans by place names. Thus, the Indians who were around the Nanticoke River were named the Nanticokes. Their dialect is related to that of the Algonquins in Canada. However, their real knowledge base derived from the Lenapes, or Delawares. *Lenape* means "the grandfather people."

Choptank probably means "it flows back strongly" in the Algonquian language, in reference to the river, the longest on Maryland's Eastern Shore.

Nanticoke means "people of the tidewaters."

Kiptopeke means "big water" and is said to be the name of an Indian who was nice to European settlers. It is now the name of a state park and town on the bay side of Virginia's Eastern Shore.

Other Native American place names from the Virginia Eastern Shore include Chincoteague, Assateague, Pungoteague, Assawoman, Onancock, and Accomack.

Wicomico is a combination of *wicko* and *mekee* and means "a place where dwellings are built." To some present-day residents of the lower Eastern Shore, the Wicomico River is affectionately called the Wicki-Mickey.

The Nanticokes called a squirrel *Little Sister*, a deer *Brother*, and an osprey *Fish Hawk*.

The Indians grew corn, squash, and beans, known to them as the *Three Sisters*.

Some indigenous Maryland tribes were the Accohannocks, Assateagues, Manokins, Nause-Waiwash, Piscataways, and Pocomokes.

Manito means "god" or "the great one."

A *powwow* is a gathering of native people, a cultural event with group singing and dancing, and artisans trading or selling native arts and crafts, including jewelry, pottery, and moccasins.

A *longhouse* is a structure built for tribal gatherings; homes are *wigwams*. The *Mound people* were the ancient ones.

trails, their names (which are on many of the rivers and towns), and their tradition as fishermen reaping the bounty of the waters throughout and around the peninsula.

Memories of slaughters and massacres also color the history of this region, and the bloodshed went both ways. Sometimes the Indians killed the settlers, and sometimes it was the other way around. At times they coexisted peacefully, even helping one another.

The Algonquins were a group of closely related Indian tribes, including the Nanticokes and Choptanks, who shared a common language. While the tribes were often competitive with or combative toward one another, they would also communicate and collaborate. In some records, these two tribes, along with the Matapeakes, are considered subtribes of the Delawares, with Algonquian as their common language. The Nanticokes were apparently the most numerous and most powerful; many Indians who remain in the area today are of Nanticoke descent.

Cambridge is the site of the last active Choptank Indian reservation in Maryland. Outside the city is an area now known as Algonquin, a spot with gorgeous views of the **Choptank River** and beautiful homes built to benefit from those views.

Prior to development, however, this area was known as the **Great Mound**, and it was a sacred place to Native Americans. One of the street names is Manito Drive, which means "god." Thus, the street name is potentially

AREA AROUND THE GREAT MOUND, NOW CALLED ALGONQUIN

sacrilegious, but no one has yet made strong objections to right that particular wrong.

To get to the Great Mound, take the first right onto Maryland Avenue after crossing the Choptank River Bridge. (If you're at the visitor center, go back to Maryland Avenue and turn right.) Follow Maryland Avenue across the Cambridge Creek Bridge and turn right onto Academy Street. Continue through the first light (Academy Street turns into Church Street after this light) and make a right at the next light onto High Street.

High Street is a paved brick street bordered on both sides with historic homes. Make a left on Water Street and follow the water along through Cambridge's charming historic district.

Water Street leads to Bellevue Avenue. At 28 Bellevue, you can view **Annie Oakley's house**, where she lived with her husband for several years while taking a hiatus from the Wild West show. Oakley used to shoot waterfowl from the second floor of the house. It's a private home now.

Continue to follow the water along Maple Avenue and then Riverside Drive, where the view is breathtaking. At the end of Riverside, turn left onto Bayview Avenue and follow it to the next stop sign. Make a right on Hambrooks Boulevard and another right on Sandy Hill Road. This is the area now known as Algonquin, previously known as the Great Mound by local Native Americans.

The Great Mound was said to have been built by the ancient ones, and Indians held ceremonies there for thousands of years until European settlers arrived in the 17th century. Water was the main mode of transportation for the Indians, and they always wanted at least two routes nearby from which to reach water. From the sacred area around the Great Mound, the Indians had the Choptank River and Jenkins Creek.

Continue on Sandy Hill Road until you reach Hataswap Circle on your right. (Hataswap was named after an old chief.) This is a residential area with large beautiful homes, and it's easy to see why the Great Mound was built here during ancient times. The river views are amazing.

If you're hungry after your driving tour, a good restaurant is **Ava's Pizzeria & Wine Bar** in Cambridge. (This is a branch of the one in St. Michaels and the food and service are just as good.) If you want to stay over, try the **Hyatt Regency Chesapeake Bay Golf Resort, Spa & Marina**. The grounds are absolutely gorgeous and there's lots to do, from swinging a golf club to shooting pool, and from lounging to reveling in spa treatments.

Native American culture. The Nanticokes were proficient at shellwork, or making wampum from large clamshells. These shells were used for decoration, jewelry, peace belts, and treaty belts. The Europeans sometimes used them as money.

In Nanticoke life, the clan system was vitally important. First allegiance

BEAUTIFUL CRAFTSMANSHIP ON DISPLAY AT NANTICOKE INDIAN MUSEUM

was always to the clan, second allegiance to the village, and third allegiance to the "chief of chiefs." At one time, the principal chief lived north of **Vienna, Maryland**, along what is now Indiantown Road.

Vienna is a town on the **Nanticoke River** where US 50 crosses the river. It was at one time the center of Nanticoke Indian territory. The river is named after the powerful Nanticoke people who navigated the river and lived on its shores.

Emperor's Landing is the current name for the town's waterfront park. The area around Vienna was an established Indian settlement and home to the tribe's chiefs (thus the adoption of the name Emperor's Landing). The feast grounds for the Nanticokes were also nearby.

To visit the **Handsell historic manor home and replica Indian longhouse**, go back out to US 50 East and take the second exit for Vienna. Make a left on MD 331. Almost directly across the road, you'll see Indiantown Road. Turn right onto Indiantown Road and continue for about 1 mile. The manor home and longhouse will be on your right. The longhouse is a scale model with fire pits, racks for sleeping, and storage.

Following the Nanticokes to Delaware. Most of the Native American history of the region is gleaned on a bits-and-pieces basis. That's partially because much of the culture is based on oral history. It's also because many Indians were dispersed to join other tribes to the north and out west. The purpose of this journey is to unearth obscure but compelling symbols and places that tell at least some of the tale. Connecting with the history that unfolded in these places is a way to preserve that history.

One place where you can find a collection of artifacts and other items is the **Nanticoke Indian Museum** in **Oak Orchard**, east of **Millsboro** in Southern Delaware.

To get to Oak Orchard from Vienna, take US 50 East to MD 353 North. After the Delaware line, the road variably becomes DE 26, DE 30, and DE 24. Stay on this road through the town of Millsboro.

The museum is at the intersection of DE 24 and DE 5 (Oak Orchard Road). European settlers allowed local Indians to move to nearby Millsboro when they were displaced elsewhere.

The museum has cultural artifacts and memorabilia from the Nanticoke tribe, or "people of the tidewaters," which is what *Nanticoke* means. The tribe was one of the largest that inhabited the area before the Europeans came and decimated the Indians with unfamiliar diseases and ran them off most of their ancestral lands. The museum helps explain the history and culture of the still-existent tribe to visitors.

The artifacts on display in this small but charming museum are mostly from elders of the tribe, several of whom still live in the area. The artifacts include arrowheads, pottery, jewelry, ax hammers, spears, and taxidermy animals. The Indians are sensitive about photography, believing that capturing an image steals a portion of the soul, which is then caught in the image. When it comes to certain animals, even taxidermy versions, the spirit of the animal may still be there, so they don't want photos taken of these animals either. Be respectful of these beliefs and ask permission before taking photos.

In addition to the museum, there is the **Nanticoke Indian Powwow**, held every September in Millsboro, during which the Nanticokes do traditional dancing and singing and perform ceremonial rituals. At the powwow, visitors can buy assorted jewelry, pottery, dreamcatchers, paintings, and Native American foods. (The Nause-Waiwash Band of Indians near Vienna, Maryland, holds a similar **Native American Festival** on a different weekend in September.)

Massacres were not uncommon, either of settlers or Indians. At **Cape Henlopen**, where the Atlantic Ocean and Delaware Bay meet, the first European settlement (later called Zwaanendael, which means "valley of the swans") was established by the Dutch in 1631 as a whaling station. Soon thereafter, all 32 settlers were massacred by local Lenni-Lenape Indians over a dispute stemming from a misunderstanding about a coat of arms mounted in the settlement.

The **Zwaanendael Museum** in **Lewes** (the seaside town next to Cape Henlopen) was built by the State of Delaware in 1931 to commemorate the 300th anniversary of that first Dutch settlement—the one in which everyone was massacred. The museum is worth a drive-by as the architecture is highly unusual for the United States. That's not surprising since it's a replica of an old town hall in Hoorn, which is in the Netherlands.

There's no entrance fee to visit the museum, but the outside architecture is much more interesting than the less-than-compelling exhibits inside.

To drive to Lewes from the Nanticoke Indian Museum in Oak Orchard, take DE 5 North to DE 404/US 9 East and onto Savannah Road. There are excellent restaurants and places to stay in Lewes. Or you can head back into Maryland from Oak Orchard by taking DE 24 West to US 113 North (Dupont Boulevard) to DE 404 West, which becomes MD 404 West. If you opt to stay in Denton at the **Best Western Denton Inn,** there are a few restaurants from which to choose—**Harry's on the Green** and **Market Street Public House.**

Indian pathways. Besides place names and crops such as corn, squash, and beans, the Indians left us their paths. These paths, or trails, followed the terrain of the Eastern Shore and tended to go north-south or east-west, depending on seasonal migrations of each particular tribe.

Paths assisted the Indians in their migrations to find food during different times of the year, but the paths also led to their demise, for the paths accommodated increasing numbers of European settlers who brought diseases, liquor, and a growing desire for land.

Tracking the Native Americans of the region isn't easy. Their burial grounds, known as ossuaries, are usually downplayed to prevent them from being desecrated for artifacts. And their history on the Eastern Shore is faint, due to their moving elsewhere or, as many did, becoming assimilated.

However faint, there is knowledge of Indian trails on the peninsula, particularly around the Choptank River and especially where it was shallow enough to wade across.

Of note is the use of old Indian trails for the Underground Railroad, which helped many African American slaves escape north from the Eastern Shore prior to emancipation, which came to Maryland slaves less than a year before the end of the Civil War. For slaves, the river was both a passageway and an obstacle. Safe crossings needed to be found at shallow points, the same places Native Americans used when traveling the region.

MD 480 (Ridgely Road) follows **St. Joan's Path**, which was originally an ancient Native American trail used by both the Choptank and Nanticoke tribes. The route is basically from what is now **Hillsboro** to **Greensboro** in Maryland, which is at the upper reaches of the Choptank River.

Drive along this road to get a feel for an area where these tribes once hunted and fished and farmed for their sustenance. It is beautiful country that bears the marks of a combination of cultures—European and Native American.

Four major Indian trails all converged in the area where Greensboro is today. At this spot, Native Americans were able to wade across the Choptank River. If you were an Indian, the biggest impediment to travel was crossing a river. Wading across was much easier than chopping down a tree and making a canoe.

Choptank probably means "it flows back strongly" in the Algonquian language, in reference to the river—the longest on Maryland's Eastern Shore. It flows 70 miles across the Delmarva Peninsula and into the Chesapeake Bay.

Hillsboro was a crossing place for the **Tuckahoe River**, a main branch of the Choptank.

At **Tuckahoe State Park** and **Adkins Arboretum**, you can get a feel for the woodlands in which the Indians hunted.

To get to Tuckahoe State Park from US 50 East, turn left onto MD 404 East. After 8 miles, turn left onto MD 480 East (Ridgely Road). Travel a short

LOOKING WEST ACROSS THE CHESAPEAKE BAY FROM MATAPEAKE AT SUNSET

distance and turn left onto Eveland Road; follow the signs to different areas of the park.

To get to Adkins Arboretum from the state park, head south on Eveland Road toward MD 404; the arboretum is on the right.

Adkins Arboretum is a 400-acre native garden and preserve adjoining Tuckahoe State Park. In the arboretum, an Eagle Scout helped create an Indian replica site with a wigwam that appeals to young children. At the site, kids can sit in a circle of log seats that form the shape of a turtle. Turtles were important to Native Americans on the Eastern Shore. There is also a log representation of a snake. The entire scene has plenty to spark the imaginations, and the playfulness, of children.

The arboretum is also a good place to get some exercise by hiking along one of the marked trails. There are even several goats (behind an electric fence). Keep children away from the fence, but they're sure to enjoy the goats' bleating and movements.

The goats at the arboretum actually earn their keep by eating through overgrown brush. They are gradually moved from area to area where the undergrowth is too thick.

Native Americans once hunted in the forests on the Eastern Shore. Some of those forests are accessible by walking trails at the Adkins Arboretum and Tuckahoe State Park.

If it walked, crawled, or flew, the Nanticokes found a use for it. They ate various kinds of animals. They also ate oysters, which were plentiful at the time, as well as crabs and all varieties of fish.

Native Americans foraged for nuts, fruits, and berries in the vast forest-lands too. *Tuckahoe* was their name for one group of edible root plants that grew expansively in the muddy soil on the banks and marshes adjacent to the Choptank River. These plants came up in the spring, when the Native Americans were usually out of dried meats and nuts stored for the winter. The roots were cleaned, mashed, and eaten.

The land in this region is fertile, so the Indians could grow corn, beans, and squash—crops they shared with the Europeans. They also shared tomatoes, sweet potatoes, and pumpkins.

A perfect view. Now that you're cognizant of the beautiful lands and waterways inhabited by the Algonquin Indians on Maryland's Eastern Shore, you can head back home across the Chesapeake Bay Bridge.

However, there's one more stop to make. If you've timed it right, it's late in the day, approaching sunset. You can see the bright sun turning orange and the Bay Bridge in front of you.

Stay alert to the last exit before the bridge, the one for MD 8 both north and south. You'll want to turn left onto Romancoke Road (MD 8 South) and go straight for a few miles. Soon you'll see a sign for Matapeake Beach.

The Matapeakes were a tribe that resided on **Kent Island**, where you're driving right now. Kent Island is between the bay and the mainland of the Eastern Shore, with Kent Narrows separating the island from the mainland.

Kent is the largest island on the Maryland Eastern Shore, and it was the site of the first British settlement in the state. Known mostly as the eastern end of the bridge, Kent Island is also a destination in and of itself. Psychologically, it may get overlooked because of the leviathan that is the bridge—the excitement, dread, fascination, and relief people feel when traveling the 4.3-mile major connector.

But back to your drive. You're going to go past the right-hand turnoff to Matapeake Beach. Keep driving for just a minute, and you'll see a sign for **Matapeake Fishing Pier**. Take that right-hand turn and follow the winding, wooded road down to the waterfront; it's not far.

As you park your car in the small parking lot, you'll see the sun setting across the bay, along with silhouettes of men, women, and teenagers with their fishing rods and cameras. Walk down to the pier to witness a fantastic and unforgettable vision.

Nothing in life is perfect, but the view at sunset from this fishing pier that extends out into the bay comes close. It's extraordinary; it's dreamlike, as if in a film. On a beautiful summer night, it is absolutely gorgeous, with the Bay Bridge standing sentry, but only as a part of the whole scene, less dominant from this pier than it is while driving on it.

Before it gets totally dark, head back, turning left onto MD 8 North. You'll go through a few lights and then turn left again onto US 50 West toward Washington, DC, and Annapolis.

The bridge is right there, while your perspective on the beauty of this land is forever altered. It's easy to imagine the Algonquin people loving this region, with its abundance of food sources; transportation routes via plentiful waterways; and, of course, the absolute natural beauty that is prevalent along thousands of miles of coastline on the Chesapeake Bay and Atlantic Ocean.

IN THE AREA

Cambridge, Maryland

Accommodations

HYATT REGENCY CHESAPEAKE BAY GOLF RESORT, SPA & MARINA. Call 410-901-1234. Website: www.hyatt.com/en-US/hotel/maryland/hyatt -regency-chesapeake-bay-golf-resort-spa-and-marina/chesa.

Attractions and Recreation

ANNIE OAKLEY'S HOUSE, private home at 28 Bellevue Avenue on Hambrooks Bay.

SAILWINDS VISITOR CENTER. Call 410-228-1000. Website: visitdorchester .org/about-dorchester/visitor-center.

Dining/Drinks

AVA'S PIZZERIA & WINE BAR. Call 443-205-4350. Website: www.avas pizzeria.com.

Denton, Maryland

Accommodations

BEST WESTERN DENTON INN. Call 410-479-8400. Website: www.best western.com/en_US/book/hotels-in-denton/best-western-denton-inn /propertyCode.21046.html.

Attractions and Recreation

ADKINS ARBORETUM, Ridgely. Call 410-634-2847. Website: www.adkins arboretum.org.

TUCKAHOE STATE PARK. Call 410-820-1668. Website: dnr.maryland.gov /publiclands/Pages/eastern/tuckahoe.aspx.

Dining/Drinks

HARRY'S FOOD & SPIRITS. Call 410-479-1919. Website: www.harrysonthe green.com. Dinner only Wednesday through Saturday.

MARKET STREET PUBLIC HOUSE. Call 410-479-4720.

Kent Island, Maryland

Attractions and Recreation

MATAPEAKE FISHING PIER.

WILLIAM PRESTON LANE, JR. MEMORIAL BRIDGE (CHESAPEAKE BAY BRIDGE). Call 1-877-229-7726 (real-time traffic information). Website: www.baybridge.maryland.gov.

Lewes, Delaware

Attractions and Recreation

ZWAANENDAEL MUSEUM. Call 302-645-1148. Website: history.delaware .gov/museums/zm/zm_main.shtml.

Millsboro, Delaware

Attractions and Recreation

NANTICOKE INDIAN MUSEUM, Oak Orchard. Call 302-945-7022. Website: www.nanticokeindians.org/page/museum.

NANTICOKE INDIAN POWWOW, held in September. Call 302-945-3400. Website: www.nanticokeindians.org/page/what-powwow.

Vienna, Maryland

Attractions and Recreation

EMPEROR'S LANDING, Waterfront Park.

HANDSELL HISTORIC MANOR HOME AND REPLICA INDIAN LONGHOUSE. Call 410-228-7458. Website: www.restorehandsell.org.

NATIVE AMERICAN FESTIVAL BY THE NAUSE-WAIWASH BAND OF INDIANS, held in September. Call 410-228-0216. Website: www.turtletracks.org.

11

VISITING ALPACAS, AMISH FARMS, AND DINOSAURS

ESTIMATED LENGTH: 300 miles round-trip

ESTIMATED TIME: 2 days

GETTING THERE: From Annapolis, start by crossing the Chesapeake Bay Bridge to the Maryland Eastern Shore. Once across the bay, stay on US 50 East for 16 miles. Turn left onto MD 404 East and right onto MD 16 South toward Preston for 4.7 miles. Make a left on Pinetown Road; the alpaca farm will be on your left in about 0.6 mile.

HIGHLIGHTS: Alpaca farm with animals appealing to young kids, hand-dipped ice cream, Amish farm community, beautiful farms, horses and buggies, quilts, furniture, Victorian architecture, dinosaur skeletons.

This is certainly a kid-friendly itinerary, but it can be adapted for an adults-only journey by shopping at some of the Amish farms or driving around Dover to see Victorian architecture instead of heading to Wilmington to see dinosaurs.

The first stop on this excursion is **Outstanding Dreams Alpaca Farm**. The beautiful faces and interesting shapes of these appealing alpacas make them immediate charmers. Originally from South America, many of these animals are thriving on a few farms in the Mid-Atlantic region. Outstanding Dreams is one of those farms, located in **Preston**, below **Denton**, in the heart of Maryland's Eastern Shore.

Visiting these cuddly looking animals is a great activity to do with children, though adults fall in love with them as well. Instead of a zoo with many animals to distract them, children (and adults) can focus on learning about

AMISH HORSE-DRAWN BUGGY

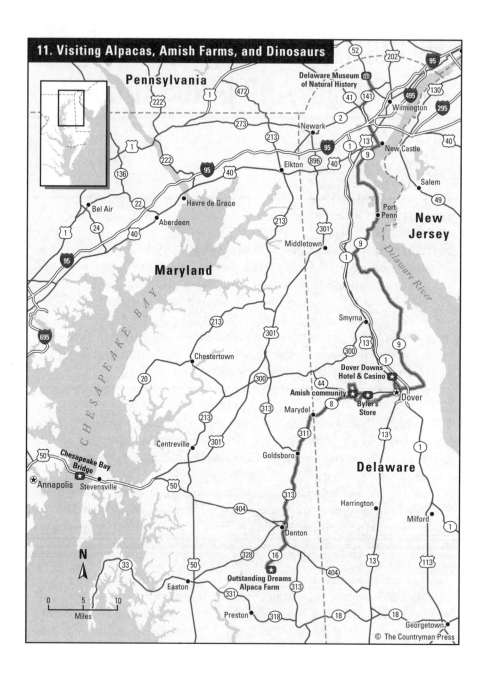

11. Visiting Alpacas, Amish Farms, and Dinosaurs

Pennsylvania

Delaware Museum of Natural History

Wilmington

Newark

New Castle

Elkton

Salem

Bel Air

Havre de Grace

Aberdeen

Middletown

Port Penn

New Jersey

Delaware River

Maryland

CHESAPEAKE BAY

Smyrna

Chestertown

Dover Downs Hotel & Casino

Amish community

Marydel

Byler's Store

Dover

Centreville

Goldsboro

Delaware

Chesapeake Bay Bridge

Annapolis   Stevensville

Harrington

Milford

N

Denton

33

Outstanding Dreams Alpaca Farm

Easton

Preston

Georgetown

0   5   10
Miles

© The Countryman Press

HORSE ON AMISH FARM

one type of animal while watching them interact with one another, eat, and cool off under a hose.

There's also an interesting gift shop on the property, with most items made from alpaca fleece turned into yarn.

The owners, Phil and Vickie Liske, are personable, and they love having visitors who want to see their alpacas. There's no charge for individuals and families who visit, and there's a reasonable fee for groups. One teacher brought 80 young students to the farm one day. Another group of 110 college students came to see the alpacas and were highly engaged as they are studying to be veterinarians. The owners are happy to have everyone from individuals to a large crowd.

Summer is the toughest time to visit because the animals are the least active due to the heat. You can visit year-round, however, and late morning is usually a good time. The Liskes just ask that you call or e-mail in advance to let them know you're coming by. According to Phil, "If we're home, we're open. But visits are by reservation only."

The Liskes will readily tell you all about their 30 or so alpacas, including the animals' names and genealogies. The males and females are kept in separately fenced areas; otherwise, it's explained,they will breed continuously.

Children are cautioned not to chase or try to scare the alpacas. Visitors of all ages are also told not to pet the animals except under the Liskes' supervision, mainly because the alpacas often don't like being petted and they are likely to spit if they feel threatened. Otherwise, they are generally gentle, and they are adorable and fascinating, whether they're eating grass, huddling around a running hose to get cool and wet, or posing for photos (especially the males, who are quite the models).

The alpacas' fleece is sheared once each year and sent to a fiber mill, where it is made into yarn. Their heads and legs are not sheared, however, but are left alone. All in all, it takes only 10 minutes for each animal to be sheared in the spring.

The owners give each alpaca a name. In their flock, some of the names are Ivory Coast, Chasin' the Dream (constantly running and nicknamed Chase), Penelope Pitstop (born at a gas station on the way to the vet), and Anticipation Annie.

Alpacas are relatives of llamas, which are beasts of burden used to carrying 300 to 500 pounds. Alpacas are smaller than llamas, however, and are bred for their fleece, which is not unlike cashmere, rather than for transporting heavy loads.

Alpacas are also related to camels. In fact, they are called New World camels.

"Little kids just crack us up asking questions like, 'How come their necks are so long?'" says Phil. "They'll also ask the difference between boy and girl alpacas; for that question I refer them to their parents.

"We love answering questions. It's a good give-and-take."

ALPACAS AT OUTSTANDING DREAMS ALPACA FARM

Alpacas originated in South America, mainly in Peru but also in Bolivia and Chile, as far back as the Inca civilization. They come in various colors, with white alpacas having the softest fleece.

Raising alpacas is mostly a cottage industry, and the Liskes, through breeding alpacas both for their fleece and to sell them to other farms, get attached to the animals. "We find it hard letting some of them go," acknowledges Phil.

The Liskes originally bought a few alpacas because they were cute and a good deal. But their farm is not a hobby for them; it's a business. They are hay dealers, and breeding alpacas is another source of revenue. "Saying goodbye is the toughest part," says Phil. "But as a business, we do have to sell."

"We made a lot of mistakes when we started in 2007. We are self-educated," Phil explains. Now experienced and wiser, they belong to the Maryland Alpaca Breeders Association and frequently advise other farmers on how to raise alpacas.

After you visit the alpaca farm, it will no doubt be lunchtime. Options include bringing a picnic lunch to eat on the grounds of the farm. Or you can go to **Market Street Public House** in Denton.

And if you want to spend the night, the only option in this extremely rural area is the **Best Western Denton Inn**, though **Easton** is only about 20 minutes away with additional options for lodging and dining.

When you're ready to leave, head to **Dover**, the capital of Delaware, to drive around the farm community settled by Amish families to the west of the city.

Most people naturally think of Lancaster, Pennsylvania, as the place to tour farmland and shops with Amish proprietors and artisans. West-central Delaware (in Kent County) is not necessarily a first or even a second thought, but it is an interesting way to go. Although there are large communities of Amish in Pennsylvania and parts of Ohio, there are also groups of Amish who live on the Western Shore in Southern Maryland and in the part of Delaware west of Dover, the state capital, which is included in this itinerary.

After you've explored this area, you can always head to Lancaster, with its larger Amish community. That's only about two hours away. But the area around Dover is enough to give you and your family an idea of how the Amish live.

From Denton, get on MD 313 North. In the town of Goldsboro, turn right onto MD 311, then take another right on MD 454 (Crown Stone Road) in **Marydel**.

Since Marydel is half in Maryland and half in Delaware (thus its name), MD 454 quickly becomes DE 8 (Halltown Road). (If you're mapping the route online or via GPS, note that DE 8 may show up as State Route 8.)

Halltown Road changes again to become Forrest Avenue. At the corner of Forrest Avenue and Rose Valley School Road is a large store with an

Amish Way of Life

Horse and buggy is the preferred method of travel for the Amish in the Dover area. If a member of the community needs to get to a job, he or she will sometimes let someone "English" pick him or her up in a car or van. However, members of the Amish community never drive motorized vehicles themselves.

You'll notice that all the white farmhouses have white curtains at the windows. You'll also notice there are no electrical or telephone wires. Instead, you'll likely see a windmill used for generating a little power.

While on the farm roads, you'll often see signs indicating various items for sale. These may include flowers, eggs, produce, handmade furniture, quilts, and other typical Amish items.

You may also see the men walking behind horse-drawn plows in the fields, young boys playing on swings, or women and their daughters sitting under a tree peeling fruit. You'll see clothes drying outside, for there are no electric or gas dryers.

There are lots of animals too, which will delight children if you're taking a family drive. There are many horses, of course, as well as chickens, roosters, cows, and goats.

---

equally large parking lot. That's officially **Byler's Store** though many refer to it as the "Country Store" or the "Amish Store." Located in the heart of an Amish community, Byler's caters to Amish as well as "English" (non-Amish) customers.

Though not Amish-owned, the store carries a lot of Amish-crafted furniture. There are also gifts and groceries, homemade jams and other foods, and marvelous hand-dipped ice cream in rotating seasonal and regular flavors. The two most popular choices are Butter Pecan and Coffee Almond Fudge. Everyone loves ice cream, so a stop at Byler's is popular. It's also a good starting point for a drive around the Amish farmlands. Keep in mind that Byler's is closed on Sunday.

In the large parking lot, you'll mostly see cars. However, there are likely to be a few horses with buggies parked in spaces with hitching posts; these are located to the left of the store as you face it from the front.

Amish buggies in Delaware are different from those you might see in the larger Amish community to the north in Lancaster, Pennsylvania. The Delaware buggies look a bit like funeral hearses.

After treating the family to ice cream (and other goodies if you want, including sandwiches), get everyone back in the car. You're going to drive around the farmland in the Amish community.

From the parking lot, take a right on Forrest Avenue. Turn left onto Sharon Hill Road and left again onto Winding Creek Road.

This will bring you back to Forrest Avenue. Turn right onto Forrest, then right onto Victory Chapel Road. Make a left on West Denneys Road, a left on Pearsons Corner Road, a left on Yoder Drive, and a left on Nault Road.

Once again, you'll come back out on Forrest Avenue (DE 8). Turn right on Forrest and right again on Rose Valley School Road.

When driving around the Amish community, take your time. This is meant to be a relaxing look at a group of people who live among us. Also, the Amish will be on foot or in horse-drawn buggies, so you will want to be aware of the need to slow down on these back roads.

There are a few hundred Amish households in the Dover area. If you see a satellite dish, antenna, or electrical lines on a house, it's not Amish.

Amish farms are well kept, with tidy gardens, white-painted houses, and often small outhouses about 20 to 40 feet away from the houses.

It's fascinating to see how differently the Amish live from most Americans, how they survive quite well without the stuff most of us have—the Internet, television, electricity, and cars. When you see Amish men, women,

About Photography

Different cultures have different views of photography. Native Americans, for example, often believe that their souls are stolen if a photo is taken of them. Many indigenous peoples of Mexico believe the same thing.

Anabaptists—such as Amish, Mennonites, and River Brethren—believe that recognizable photos of people are boastful and self-centered representations. In their faiths, they adhere to humility with a focus on community; thus, snapping photos of their faces is disrespectful of their religious beliefs.

There's another aspect to this too. Unwanted photos are clearly intrusive, especially if taken due to unfamiliarity with someone's culture and unusual clothing.

The Amish and other sects are entitled to their beliefs and their privacy. Thus, a caution: Visitors should not take photos of people's faces without respectfully asking, and receiving, permission. This is a good practice to use with cultures around the world, and doing so makes it more likely you'll capture smiles rather than frowns.

This is definitely a factor when photographing the Amish in Delaware, Maryland, and Pennsylvania. Taking an unobtrusive distant shot of their farmland or horse-drawn buggies, however, is usually acceptable.

COASTAL DELAWARE

and children, they are not on cell phones; they are not texting or Googling or taking photos.

The Amish live with us, next to us. But their lives are simpler. Even though modern conveniences make our lives easier, they also make them more complex.

At this point, you're on Rose Valley School Road. If this is an adults-only journey, you might want to wander around the Victorian district of the city of Dover. To do so, proceed on Rose Valley School Road and turn left onto Hazletville Road. As you go over the railroad tracks, Hazletville turns into North Street. Stay on North Street, then turn left onto South State Street.

The neighborhood with the most spectacular Victorian houses is located in a condensed area of State Street from North Street to Silver Lake; this area covers approximately 11 blocks.

If you want even more adult entertainment, spend the night at **Dover Downs Hotel & Casino**, where you can gamble, dine at **Michele's** or one of the other restaurants, and drink. Dover Downs is right on US 13 (DuPont Highway).

If this is a family outing, instead of driving around the Victorian district, from DE 8 go east until you reach US 13 or, for a longer ride, DE 9. Once you reach one of these highways, travel north toward **Wilmington.**

If you decide to spend the night in Dover, you might want to take the longer, more picturesque and isolated drive on DE 9 along the coast the next day.

On US 13 North, you'll see a commercial corridor from the highway. On DE 9 North, you'll be driving past wildlife areas and bay beaches, with glimpses of Delaware Bay.

If you take DE 9, stop for a few minutes in **Port Penn** to enjoy this village where the Delaware River and Delaware Bay meet. There are marshlands and many ghost stories here. Port Penn was once a thriving port, but it declined after it was bypassed by the C&D Canal in 1829 (it's below the canal) and by the railroad in 1858. The village is quaint and has a tiny museum inside a former schoolhouse.

Whether you take DE 9 or US 13, at **New Castle** you'll want to get on DE 141/US 202 heading north. Take the exit for DE 52 North and drive toward Greenville for about 2 miles on Kennett Pike. The **Delaware Museum of Natural History** will be on your left.

After seeing alpacas and driving around the Amish countryside outside Dover, you may want to make this additional stop if you're traveling with kids. Luckily, Delaware is a small state geographically, and Dover isn't far from Wilmington.

The Delaware Museum of Natural History is a fascinating place for adults and kids alike. The skeletons of two dinosaurs, 150 million years old, are dramatic, as are the taxidermy exhibits about other animals. The interactive displays are excellent too. Jurassic Park kind of comes alive, in a gentle way, here.

After you've looked at, and talked about, various animals with your kids, it will be time to head out. To make the trip home more interesting, visit the museum gift shop, which sells books and toys to further stimulate young minds and emotions. And if you get hungry, nearby **Big Fish Grill** is a good spot for the family.

On leaving, follow DE 52 back to DE 141 to I-95, at which point you can head south toward Baltimore and Washington, DC.

IN THE AREA

Denton, Maryland

Accommodations

BEST WESTERN DENTON INN. Call 410-479-8400. Website: www
.bestwestern.com/en_US/book/hotels-in-denton/best-western-denton-inn
/propertyCode.21046.html.

Attractions and Recreation

OUTSTANDING DREAMS ALPACA FARM, Preston. Call 410-673-2002 or
410-829-4492 (Phil's cell). Website: www.outstandingdreamsfarm.com.

Dining/Drinks

MARKET STREET PUBLIC HOUSE. Call 410-479-4720.

Dover, Delaware

Accommodations

DOVER DOWNS HOTEL & CASINO. Call 302-674-4600 or 1-800-711-5882.
Website: www.doverdowns.com.

Attractions and Recreation

BYLER'S STORE, West Dover. Call 302-674-1689. Website: www.bylers.com.

Dining/Drinks

MICHELE'S AT DOVER DOWNS. Call 302-857-2120. Website: www.dover
downs.com/dining/restaurants/Micheles.

Wilmington, Delaware

Attractions and Recreation

DELAWARE MUSEUM OF NATURAL HISTORY. Call 302-658-9111. Website: www.delmnh.org.

Dining/Drinks

BIG FISH GRILL. Call 302-652-3474. Website: www.bigfishriverfront.com.

12

TRAVERSING THE BANKS OF THE C&D CANAL

ESTIMATED LENGTH: 220 miles round-trip from Baltimore (plus a few nautical miles)

ESTIMATED TIME: 2–3 days

GETTING THERE: From Baltimore, take I-95 North to exit 109. Take MD 279 toward Elkton. At the intersection with MD 213, turn left and head south. The north side of Chesapeake City is right before the canal bridge, and the south side can be accessed immediately on the southern end of the bridge.

HIGHLIGHTS: The charming town of Chesapeake City with shops and B&Bs, Delaware City, ferry to Pea Patch Island and Fort Delaware, C&D Canal Museum, C&D Recreation Trail, New Castle, University of Delaware's main campus in Newark.

You can actually start out at either end of the canal—in **Chesapeake City, Maryland,** or in **Delaware City, Delaware.** There's no easy way to drive along the banks of the canal by car, but the recreation trail on the canal's northern bank is great for hikers and bikers. The trail runs approximately 14.5 miles from North Chesapeake City to Delaware City, though varying lengths are reported by different sources. Perhaps to some it seems a bit longer when they get tired. The 1.8 miles of trail on the Maryland side constitute the Ben Cardin Trail. The 12.7 miles on the other side of the Delaware border constitute the Michael Castle Trail. Castle is a former Delaware governor and US congressman who helped initiate the project in Congress. Cardin is the Senator from Maryland who helped make the trail a reality.

For this itinerary, we'll start out in Chesapeake City because it's the more

WILLIAM PENN STATUE IN THE HEART OF NEW CASTLE

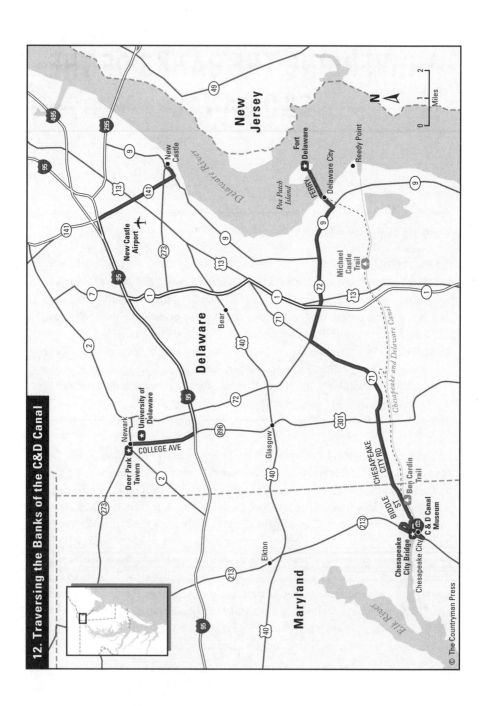

© The Countryman Press

dramatic end of the canal. Besides, *C* comes before *D*. You can reverse the order if you like.

Also, technically Delaware City is no longer the eastern terminus. In 1927, the Army Corps of Engineers made a sea-level entrance to the canal at **Reedy Point**, 2 miles south of the original terminus at Delaware City.

But Delaware City is still the romantic end of the canal. In Delaware City, however, you should not expect to see large ships other than those out on the river, perhaps on their way to or from Reedy Point.

The history of the **Chesapeake & Delaware (C&D) Canal** is fascinating. It took 26 years of intensive manual labor to dig the canal, which was finally ready for business in 1829. Even though the land distance between the Delaware River and Chesapeake Bay is only 14 miles where the canal is located, digging that much ground by hand was an expensive and time-consuming project accomplished before modern equipment was available.

Prior to the canal's existence, transporting goods by boat from Philadelphia to Baltimore required a long trip around the Delmarva Peninsula, with the route including the **Delaware River**, **Delaware Bay**, **Atlantic Ocean**, and the **Chesapeake Bay** (unless ground transportation was used too).

More dredging was done in 1927 to convert the C&D Canal to a sea-level operation, eliminating the lock system previously in place and moving the eastern terminus to Reedy Point.

One of the busiest canals in the United States, the C&D is operated by the

CHESAPEAKE CITY BRIDGE IN THE BACKGROUND

US Army Corps of Engineers. As a major shortcut, it eliminates 300 miles from the water route between Philadelphia and Baltimore.

Ships go in both directions on the canal. Going east to west, the route includes the Delaware River, the C&D Canal, the **Elk River**, and finally the Chesapeake Bay; going the other way, the bodies of water are obviously reversed.

If you want to learn more about the canal, stop in at the **C&D Canal Museum** in Chesapeake City.

And if your timing's right, you'll see huge container ships casting a dark shadow on the town as they take this shortcut between the Delaware River and Chesapeake Bay. The busiest days are unpredictable, however, so when you visit you might see only small recreational boats out on the canal.

Like the Chesapeake Bay Bridge, Chesapeake City is considered a gateway to Maryland's Eastern Shore, in this case from I-95, which traverses the Eastern Seaboard from New England to Florida.

Located approximately halfway between Philadelphia and Baltimore, the town is small but perfect for a day trip or weekend getaway. If you like to draw or paint, there are lovely spots on the southern bank under the shadow of the bridge where you can set up an easel or open up a sketchpad.

Tucked under the high majestic bridge, the town of **Chesapeake City** was once called the village of Bohemia. Besides being part of a major shipping passageway, the town is delightful for visitors, with its inns, specialty and antiques shops, historic canal museum, seasonal boat tours, and waterfront restaurants. Places to stay include the **Elk Forge Bed & Breakfast** (close to nearby Elkton) and **Ship Watch Inn Bed & Breakfast**; places to dine include **The Bayard House Restaurant**, **Schaefer's Restaurant & Canal Bar**, and **Chesapeake Inn Restaurant & Marina**.

Chesapeake City is completely walkable, as it's really village-size. The main attraction, besides the canal, is definitely the dramatically high bridge, which replaced a lower one destroyed when a ship rammed into it in 1942.

After that accident, a ferry was the only way to get from one side of town to the other; that predicament lasted for seven years. The new bridge was put into operation in 1949.

To drive from Chesapeake City to Delaware City, head east on Cecil Street and continue onto Union Street. Turn left onto Biddle Street for about 2 miles and enter Delaware. Continue onto Chesapeake City Road for a little more than 2 miles. Turn right onto DE 71 North (Red Lion Road) for 4 miles. Turn right onto DE 72 South (Wrangle Hill Road) for 1.5 miles.

Take a slight left to stay on DE 72 South and stay on Wrangle Hill Road another 2.3 miles. Continue onto DE 9 South (Fifth Street) for 1.3 miles, then turn left onto Clinton Street for 0.5 mile.

To walk or bike the trail on the northern bank, turn east just north of the bridge and find parking. Just remember you'll have to walk or ride back the same number of miles, so don't let yourself get too tired. During the summer a ferry runs between north and south Chesapeake City; if it's scheduled to run you can park on either side of the canal.

Delaware City, at the other (previous) end of the canal, is similar to Chesapeake City in that it's easy to find amateur painters sitting in front of an easel in this town as well. But it's even more of a sleepy little town than Chesapeake City, and it's where you can depart by ferry for a visit to **Fort Delaware** on **Pea Patch Island**, which is a Delaware state park.

The fort was built in the 1800s to protect Philadelphia and Wilmington from invasion. It was later used to house Confederate army prisoners during the Civil War. Although it was originally built as a defensive fort to keep people out, not in, the island proved to be a good place to keep prisoners, for not many managed to escape.

Around the fort is a wet ditch, which was used for catching and containing human waste. It also discouraged anyone from breaching the fort. It looks like a moat, but that would belong outside a castle, not a fort.

Located 44 miles south of Philadelphia on the Delaware River, the fort is open every day from Memorial Day to Labor Day except in bad weather; no one wants to ride a ferry in a storm anyway. Assuming you're out and about because the weather is conducive, it's likely the ferry is operating. Once you

FORT DELAWARE ON PEA PATCH ISLAND

get to the island, little jitneys (or trams) drive you the short distance to the fort on a rather bumpy road through marshland.

Historic role players are often dull, but the "actors" at the fort are quite articulate and knowledgeable. Once there, you should take at least one 20-minute tour with a living-history interpreter. Aspects of the architecture, like angles in walls created to deflect cannonballs, are interesting, especially to those intrigued by military history.

Though it is not as dramatic as a visit to Alcatraz off the shore of San Francisco, a tour of Fort Delaware still provides insights into the trials and tribulations of life on an island being used as a prison—for the prisoners as well as their captors.

On Pea Patch Island, everyone was confined on less than 75 acres in rather unbearable conditions. Isolation and issues of sanitation and deprivation were prevalent. Today there are problems with bats and a disease they carry. Not an ideal place then or now.

After the ferry ride back to Delaware City, and while you're in the area, head up to historic **New Castle**, where a **statue of William Penn** in the center of the town square is a clue to the town's history. As you walk around town, you'll see little raised concrete blocks next to the curbs—reminders of a time when people needed to step up to climb into carriages or onto horses.

In New Castle, you'll see British flags flying next to American ones, proof that we're now at peace with the country against which we fought so hard to gain our independence. The Revolutionary War is long over.

To get to New Castle from Delaware City, take DE 72 to DE 1 to I-95 North to DE 141 East, crossing over US 13. Bear left onto DE 9, then turn right onto Delaware Street.

After a quick tour of the green and the wonderful views of the Delaware River, leave New Castle and head to **Newark** (the Delaware city of that name, not the one in New Jersey), home to the main campus of the **University of Delaware** (UD).

Newark, Delaware, is pronounced *new-ark,* not *new-wurk,* like the city in New Jersey. To get to Delaware's Newark from New Castle, take DE 9 to DE 141 West, crossing US 13. Travel south on I-95. Take the exit for DE 896 North and follow South College Avenue into downtown Newark.

Once in Newark, you'll be delighted by **Caffé Gelato** on East Main Street. The city is crowded even during summer when school's out, but it's worth fighting a few blocks of traffic to have lunch (or dinner) there. The food and service are excellent. And gelato, or Italian-style ice cream, is a must for dessert. Their version is nearly as good as you'd get in Venice, Italy.

UD is the largest university in Delaware, and it has an expansive main campus here, so drive around a little. College towns are infinitely intriguing,

CAFFÉ GELATO IN NEWARK, DELAWARE

as they are the starting point for so many young adult lives. Newark is the place thousands get an education, pursue grown-up social lives, and cheer for the university's sports teams.

UD is the alma mater of former Baltimore Ravens quarterback Joe Flacco, who helped put UD's Blue Hens on the sports map and led the Ravens to a Super Bowl victory in February 2013 to end the 2012 season.

Edgar Allan Poe once spent a week lecturing on poetry at Newark Academy, a private school that was part of the entity that morphed into the University of Delaware. The **Deer Park Tavern** was supposedly one of Poe's watering holes when he was in town.

The Deer Park was also the site of an inn, at the time called St. Patrick's Inn, where Charles Mason and Jeremiah Dixon reportedly stayed during one phase of working with their team of surveyors to determine and mark the boundary between Pennsylvania and Maryland.

Deer Park Tavern is still serving patrons at its location on West Main Street near UD. There are reports the tavern was also once a stop on the Underground Railroad, assisting slaves to reach freedom.

From Newark, drive back to Baltimore via I-95 South.

IN THE AREA

Chesapeake City, Maryland

Accommodations

ELK FORGE BED & BREAKFAST, outside nearby Elkton. Call 410-392-9007. Website: www.elkforge.com.

SHIP WATCH INN BED & BREAKFAST. Call 410-885-5300. Website: www .shipwatchinn.com.

Attractions and Recreation

BEN CARDIN TRAIL.

C&D CANAL MUSEUM. Call 410-885-5621. Website: chesapeakecity.com /cd-canal-museum.

Dining/Drinks

THE BAYARD HOUSE RESTAURANT. Call 410-885-5040.

CHESAPEAKE INN RESTAURANT & MARINA. Call 410-885-2040. Website: www.chesapeakeinn.com.

SCHAEFER'S RESTAURANT & CANAL BAR. Call 410-885-7200. Website: schaeferscanalhouse.com.

Delaware City, Delaware

Attractions and Recreation

FORT DELAWARE, via ferry to Pea Patch Island. Call 302-834-7941. Website: delawarestateparks.reserveamerica.com/tourList.do.

MICHAEL CASTLE TRAIL.

Newark, Delaware

Attractions and Recreation

UNIVERSITY OF DELAWARE (MAIN CAMPUS). Call 302-831-2792. Website: www.udel.edu.

Dining/Drinks

CAFFÉ GELATO. Call 302-738-5811. Website: www.caffegelato.net.

DEER PARK TAVERN. Call 302-369-9414. Website: www.deerparktavern .com.

New Castle, Delaware

Attractions and Recreation

WILLIAM PENN STATUE.

13

TRACKING THE WAR OF 1812

ESTIMATED LENGTH: 360 miles round-trip from Annapolis

ESTIMATED TIME: 3–4 days

GETTING THERE: From the Baltimore and Annapolis area, take US 50 East across
the Chesapeake Bay Bridge toward Easton. Turn right onto MD 322 (Easton
Bypass). Drive 4 miles and turn right again onto MD 33 (St. Michaels Road) to
the town of St. Michaels. On your right, just past the Chesapeake Bay Maritime Museum, is the entrance to the Inn at Perry Cabin.

HIGHLIGHTS: St. Michaels, Inn at Perry Cabin, Tilghman Island, Taylors Island,
Cannonball House Maritime Museum in Lewes.

In 1812, the British ruled the seas and had the strongest, most powerful navy in the world. When the United States declared war on Great Britain, British naval superiority was a fact.

The Chesapeake Bay, with its access to Baltimore and proximity to the nation's capital, along with its role as a major commercial waterway, made it a natural battleground.

Baltimore and Washington were targets on the Western Shore, but the Eastern Shore saw its share of the war too. The British blockaded the bay, pilfered food and other supplies, attacked towns and villages, and occupied some territory.

Twice the British attacked the town of **St. Michaels**, which is part of the reason this journey leads us there. The other part is that St. Michaels is a thoroughly delightful town on the **Miles River**, with lovely places to stay, dine, shop, and sail.

Perhaps a more obvious starting point for a journey to learn about the

HIDDEN DOORWAY BEHIND A BOOKCASE AT THE INN AT PERRY CABIN

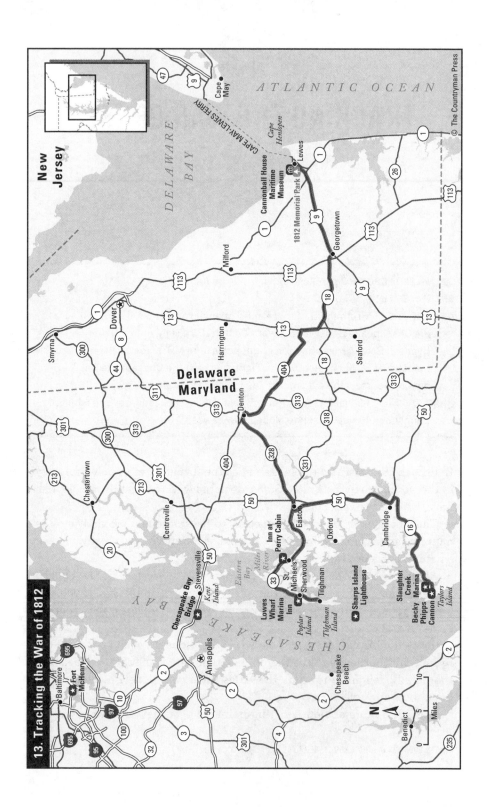

13. Tracking the War of 1812

War of 1812 is the city of **Baltimore**. Though not a back road and not on the Eastern Shore, Baltimore played a vital role in the War of 1812—or at least a memorable one. **Fort McHenry** and the origins of "The Star-Spangled Banner" are well-documented history.

However, when one talks to residents farther down the bay in Southern Maryland on the Western Shore, they often refer to what happened in Baltimore as a "small battle." They make this statement in comparison to the down-and-out naval battle that occurred in **St. Leonard Creek** on the **Patuxent River**. The St. Leonard Creek battle occurred after a month or so of cat-and-mouse incursions between the Americans and the British forces that sailed on warships up the Chesapeake to the Patuxent.

When 3,500 British troops disembarked in the town of **Benedict**, with its tiny population of about 300 residents, the British pilfered just about everything that was not nailed down.

The importance of these struggles is profound even though the Americans were unable to stop the British from subsequently marching on to Washington, DC, where they burned down many buildings, including the White House and US Capitol.

While a local militia was not enough to thwart thousands of seasoned British troops, elsewhere along the waterways Americans ultimately managed to repel the Brits, including in some places on the Eastern Shore.

We're starting from Baltimore, where Fort McHenry proudly displays the flag on the hill, and driving over the Chesapeake Bay Bridge. We're going to St. Michaels, in a wealthy and beautiful part of the state, to an ultimately delightful resort—**Inn at Perry Cabin**.

When people think of the War of 1812 in Maryland, they often overlook the battles, skirmishes, and raids that took place on the Eastern Shore, starting in 1813. Those are some of the military engagements this trip is meant to uncover. Along the way, you'll see lovely countryside, and you will have a good time. After all, the war is long past.

Location, location, location. This expression is generally used for residential and commercial real estate. But it's no less important, vital even, in times of war.

The War of 1812 was no exception. Whoever controlled the waterways of the Chesapeake Bay was in a strong position to control war in the region.

With **Kent, Poplar, Tilghman, and Sharps Islands** captured by the British, St. Michaels was the next obvious battleground. The Americans managed to thwart the British at St. Michaels not once but twice. The town took fire during an attack that occurred in August 1813 and repelled the Brits again about two weeks later when they landed at Wades Point, 5 miles outside town.

Location is also important when it comes to travel and relaxation.

With a stellar reputation, it might be expected that the Inn at Perry Cabin would disappoint. After all, no place is that great. Or is it? From the moment you drive up the impressive tree-lined drive and observe the casually dressed guests wandering the beautiful gardens, you are likely to smile.

There are certainly more elaborate hotels in the world, all more resplendent, more opulent, and more regal. Yet on the Maryland Eastern Shore, the Inn at Perry Cabin is the ultimate resort, situated next to **Fogg's Cove** and the Miles River and hugging the shoreline with its manicured lawns and Adirondack chairs. It's also right next door to the **Chesapeake Bay Maritime Museum**.

Perhaps the loveliest aspect of the inn is the quiet—true quiet that is charming in its simplicity. In 1813, there may have been fighting. Now all is tranquil.

There's a spa and a pool, six gardens, and bikes you can borrow, plus a dock with kayaks, fishing boats, and sailing lessons.

To ignore the water would seem absurd. If you sit on your balcony or on the lawn reading a novel while facing the water, you're acknowledging the powerful allure that water has had for all civilizations—as the source of life, of sustenance, and of marvelous fish and seafood.

Relax and enjoy the small moments, like being lazy in the sun or laughing over a funny story someone in your family shares over breakfast. Talking about everything and nothing is what it's all about. The Inn at Perry Cabin is a major inspiration—it sets the scene while you and your loved ones provide a dialogue unique unto yourselves.

With regard to food from the local waterways, the restaurant at the inn, **Stars**, serves an abundance of fish and seafood. Unfortunately, the cedar and herb rolls, wickedly addictive, are no longer part of the cuisine. Miss Gussie, who made them for years, has sadly passed away.

Even if you have no desire to read while you're here, don't miss a stop at the inn's library just off the reception area. There's a hidden doorway behind one of the bookcases that leads into a lovely morning room. Wouldn't we all want to have a secret entrance to such a room?

The hidden door is original to the house, built not long after the end of the Civil War. In tumultuous times, secret passageways and exits would likely have come in handy. If nothing else, it is a fascinating curiosity.

Several moviemakers have used the local area for filming. The Inn at Perry Cabin was the setting for *Wedding Crashers* with Vince Vaughn and Owen Wilson, and nearby **Oxford** was used for *Failure to Launch* with Sarah Jessica Parker and Matthew McConaughey.

Dining at Perry Cabin is lovely. You will also want to have a meal in town at **Ava's Pizzeria & Wine Bar**, where the pasta and seafood dishes are superb.

The British in the Chesapeake. You can, of course, stay put at the Inn at Perry Cabin and have a lovely time, perhaps borrow one of the bikes to ride into town and do a bit of shopping, or go out of the resort to have some meals in St. Michaels or nearby Easton.

Or you can take some drives to see more War of 1812 territorial history. The closest drive is to **Tilghman Island**.

Luckily, Tilghman Island retains its authenticity as a lovely watermen's community. A portion of Tilghman was occupied by the British in 1813 and 1814; the British even built two barracks to house their troops there. It's hard to imagine this lovely community occupied by foreign troops, but it happened.

If you've never been to Tilghman, take the opportunity to visit when you're in nearby St. Michaels, for it's special and no more than a 25-minute drive away.

Water defines Tilghman, from its small land mass that's virtually all coastline to the watermen who make the island their home. It is no wonder the British showed up here in force. Besides its requisite workboats, Tilghman provides lots of recreation—from sailing to fishing to touring and just relaxing.

Drive down the island to the southern tip, where there's a spot favored by some local fishermen and a view of distant **Sharps Island Lighthouse** out in the bay.

Sharps Island has actually disappeared, completely eroded away. At one time, it measured about 900 acres, and the present caisson lighthouse was erected in 1882. Now all that's left is the tilted lighthouse, knocked off center by an ice floe. But the island was there in April 1813 when British troops landed.

On your way back to St. Michaels, make a left turn at **Sherwood** onto Lowes Wharf Road and drive to the bay. From **Lowes Wharf Marina Inn and Restaurant** at the end of the road, you can just see **Poplar Island**, or what is left of it, on the horizon.

Poplar was on the British attack route during the War of 1812. The British took it over and used it as a staging area.

In the 1800s, Poplar encompassed more than 1,000 acres, but by the 1990s extensive erosion and a rising sea level had reduced it to less than 10 acres.

The US Army Corps of Engineers is currently rebuilding the island, acre by acre, to create a wildlife and bird sanctuary—a project scheduled to be completed in 2041. To reconstruct the island, the corps is using material dredged from clearing deep shipping channels that lead to Baltimore (so ships of ever-increasing size can continue using the channels).

Drive to Taylors Island. From St. Michaels, take MD 33 East and turn right onto Easton Parkway. Take the ramp onto US 50 East to a right on MD 16 West (Church Creek Road). Follow MD 16 West for 16 miles to Taylors Island.

The Battle of the Ice Mound took place off the northern tip of **Taylors Island** on **James Island** outside the village of Madison, which was called Tobacco Stick at that time.

During February 1815, the British vessel HMS *Dauntless* was anchored off James Island, where it got stuck in the ice. The ship was weighed down with goods the British seamen had pilfered from nearby farms.

A militia-like group of Americans was able to engage the icebound ship's tender (a smaller boat attached to the larger one for the purpose of ferrying people to shore). The Americans were successful in getting the British on board to surrender.

While taking the men into custody, the Americans were also able to release a black woman named Becky, who had been captured by the British and forced to work as the ship's cook. She was brought ashore by the militia and released.

On Taylors Island Road, there's the **Becky Phipps Cannon**, captured by the local citizens during that battle. The cannon is located by the side of the road just after you cross Slaughter Creek Bridge. It's named for Becky and Lieutenant Matthew Phibbs, commander of the British tender that was captured by the Americans; his likely misspelled name is immortalized on the cannon along with hers.

Taylors Island is about 8 miles long and 2 miles wide, with the Little Choptank River to the north, Slaughter Creek to the east, the bay to the west, and Hooper Island to the south. From parts of Taylors Island you can see Calvert Cliffs across the bay on the Western Shore.

There's not much left of James Island, which is north of Taylors Island. But back during the War of 1812, James Island was connected to Taylors Island; you could travel by road from James Island to Hooper Island, with Taylors in between.

Unfortunately, erosion has nearly destroyed James Island, and the road leading to it is long gone into the bay. No one has lived there since 1960.

If you're hungry when you're visiting Taylors Island, you're close to **Palm Beach Willie's,** a floating restaurant on Taylors Island Road that used to be a Coast Guard station in Florida. It's located on a barge in **Slaughter Creek Marina**. The name of the marina sounds a bit ominous, but it's a good place to dine—though if the weather is rough, the building sways. Of course, that's part of its charm.

Tangier Island—another island under siege. After the British burned Washington, DC, in 1814, they consolidated their fleet—an armada of 50 ships—at Tangier Island. From there they sailed north to attack Baltimore, a battle the British lost.

On the Delaware Bay. If you want a longer day trip from St. Michaels, you can drive across the Delmarva Peninsula to **Lewes**, Delaware, about 75 miles each way. To reach Lewes, take MD 33 East to MD 328 North to MD 404 East. Cross the Delaware state line and stay on DE 404 East into Lewes (pronounced *lew-is*, not *looz*).

British vessels blockaded the mouth of the Delaware Bay during the War of 1812, just as they did the Chesapeake Bay. The mouth of the Delaware Bay is at **Cape Henlopen**, with the seaside town of Lewes adjacent to it. Lewes received heavy cannon fire, with volunteers protecting the town.

Like St. Michaels, Lewes has charming shops with products that run the gamut from gourmet chocolates to jewelry made of sea glass. Lewes is even a bit more upscale, with good small hotels

CANNONBALL LODGED IN THE CANNONBALL HOUSE MARITIME MUSEUM

like **The Inn at Canal Square**, although there's nothing as special as the Inn at Perry Cabin.

In Lewes, the **Cannonball House Maritime Museum** was struck by British cannon fire in 1813 during a sustained bombardment. There's even a cannonball sticking out of the front edifice, providing its current name. No worries, though; apparently, it's not the kind of weapon that will accidentally detonate.

This nautical history museum is worth a visit if for no other reason than to see exhibits on how volunteer militia defended the town until the war ended in 1815. There's a small admission fee, but the museum is worth the expense.

Lewes's **1812 Memorial Park** sits on Front Street across from the post office. Some of the guns in the park date to the militia's defense of the town.

The British finally went home at the end of the war. Now the Americans and British are allies. It's amazing what a century or two will do.

IN THE AREA

Baltimore, Maryland

Attractions and Recreation

FORT MCHENRY NATIONAL MONUMENT AND HISTORIC SHRINE.
Call 410-962-4290. Website: www.nps.gov/fomc.

Lewes, Delaware

Accommodations

THE INN AT CANAL SQUARE. Call 302-644-3377 or 1-888-644-1911. Website: www.theinnatcanalsquare.com.

Attractions and Recreation

CANNONBALL HOUSE MARITIME MUSEUM. Call 302-645-7670. Website: www.historiclewes.org/buildings/cannonball-house.

1812 MEMORIAL PARK, Front Street.

St. Michaels, Maryland

Accommodations

INN AT PERRY CABIN. Call 410-745-2200 or 1-888-805-8885. Website: www.innatperrycabin.com.

Attractions and Recreation

CHESAPEAKE BAY MARITIME MUSEUM. Call 410-745-2916. Website: www.cbmm.org.

Dining/Drinks

AVA'S PIZZERIA & WINE BAR. Call 410-745-3081. Website: www.avas
pizzeria.com.

STARS, at Inn at Perry Cabin. Call 410-745-2200. Website: www.innat
perrycabin.com.

Sherwood, Maryland

Dining/Drinks

LOWES WHARF MARINA INN AND RESTAURANT. Call 410-745-0119.
Website: www.loweswharf.com.

Taylors Island, Maryland

Attractions and Recreation

BECKY PHIPPS CANNON, Taylors Island Road.

Dining/Drinks

PALM BEACH WILLIE'S. Call 410-221-5111. Website: www.palmbeach
willies.com.

Tilghman Island, Maryland

Attractions and Recreation

SHARPS ISLAND LIGHTHOUSE.

14

HUNTING FOR SHIPWRECK TREASURES, SEASHELLS, AND SEA GLASS

ESTIMATED LENGTH: 400 miles round-trip from Washington, DC

ESTIMATED TIME: 2–3 days

GETTING THERE: From Washington, DC, take US 50 East across the Chesapeake Bay Bridge. Continue on US 50 East/US 301 North for 10 miles until they split, at which point you want to stay to the right on US 50 East (Ocean Gateway). Continue on US 50 about 7 miles, then turn left onto MD 404 East toward the Delaware beaches, where the treasure hunting will begin.

As you travel through Denton and cross into Delaware, notice the many well-kept farms. Stay alert, as DE 404 East is winding and a bit tricky as you head toward Lewes. For a long stretch, headlights are required, even during daylight.

DE 1 and MD 528, also known as the Coastal Highway, is a giant commercial strip of stores, fast-food restaurants, gasoline stations, and motels that runs north-south and connects all the Atlantic coast beach towns.

HIGHLIGHTS: Coin Beach, DiscoverSea Shipwreck Museum, Treasures of the Sea Exhibit, shopping in Lewes and St. Michaels for sea glass, metal detecting on the beach, bargain hunting at mega outlet malls.

During this itinerary, you will master the art of getting lost—in the beauty, in the tranquility, in the fascinating history of the Atlantic coast—and then do something unusual and captivating.

Finding lost treasure—whether it's pirates' pieces of eight that wash up on the sand, bits of polished sea glass shining in the sunlight, or a country road with an abandoned sweet potato barn and an old relic of a cemetery—is a dream for many of us. So why not pursue the dream . . . just for fun?

COLLECTION OF SEA GLASS

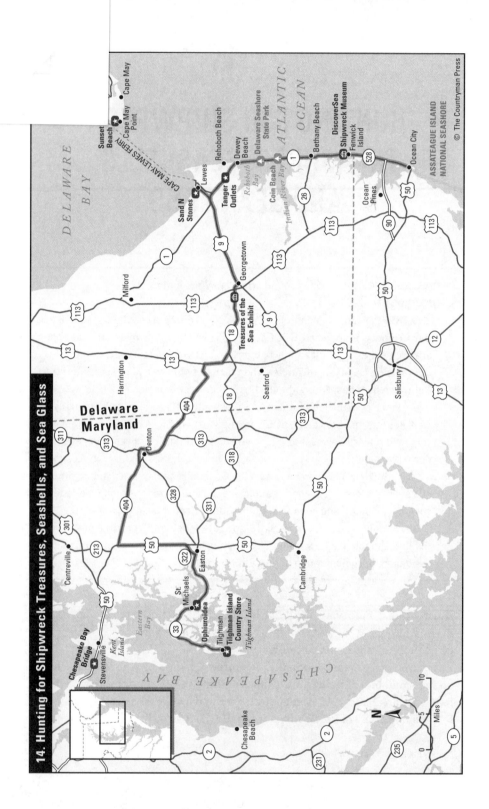

14. Hunting for Shipwreck Treasures, Seashells, and Sea Glass

© The Countryman Press

Where there is extensive shipping, there are probably lots of shipwrecks, as there were on the Delaware coast before the advent of modern weather warnings and navigational equipment. The gold and much of the other treasure that went down with these ships over the centuries did not disintegrate. Therefore, anything that has yet to be uncovered may still surface. After a nor'easter or hurricane, treasure hunters, if they're smart and very, very lucky, can end up with a remnant from a downed ship's cargo, maybe even some pieces of gold.

Gold bars, silver and gold coins, jewelry, Colombian emeralds … the possibilities are exciting. Actually finding a piece of treasure is unlikely but not impossible.

Besides gold and silver, jewels, and other valuables, glass weathered by the wind and water has both intrinsic and monetary value.

Throw a bottle into a river. It travels to an estuary (or bay) and out to sea. Decades later, it finds itself back on land, this time on a sandy beach or covered by shallow water in the surf. The glass is polished smooth now, thanks to Mother Nature—no longer a broken shard, but a smooth piece of glass that's often the size of a large coin or marble.

If it looks cloudy or opaque, you may have found a piece of sea glass.

Sea glass, driftwood, sharks' teeth, and seashells are fun to find and collect. They can be made into jewelry and used as interior design knickknacks. Collecting them, whether it's one morning after a storm or throughout a lifetime of beach vacations, is a great family activity that creates memories—memories that children will treasure when they're older and likely replicate with their own kids.

After all, everybody has fun finding stuff. Some hunt through antiques stores, others in the sand.

Since all the beach resorts are close to one another, you can stay at any of them—Rehoboth Beach, Dewey Beach, Bethany Beach, and Fenwick Island in Delaware or Ocean City in Maryland. **The Inn at Canal Square** in **Lewes** is a good bet if you don't mind driving to the beach to do your treasure hunting. If you'd rather just walk outside your hotel with the beach right there, the **Boardwalk Plaza Hotel** in **Rehoboth Beach** is a good choice. If you're traveling on a summer weekend, there will be tons of traffic up and down DE 1. If you're visiting midweek or off-season, traffic is less of an issue.

To get yourself in the mood to look for treasure, visit one or both of the local shipwreck museums.

The **DiscoverSea Shipwreck Museum** is easy to find, right on DE 1 in **Fenwick Island** above a gift shop, SeaShell City. This is an entertaining little museum for anyone interested in learning about treasures recovered from the sea, including some found along the coast of Delaware. Retrieved gold, silver, weapons, and gems are all on display.

Owner Dale W. Clifton Jr. is often on hand to tell captivating stories

TREASURES OF THE SEA EXHIBIT

about his personal adventures finding treasures from various shipwrecks. Clifton is quite the storyteller, and he'll have you wanting to try your own luck hunting for riches trapped on the ocean floor.

Clifton is a treasure hunter who believes he shakes hands with history. His stories alone are treasures, and he says that you never know what you're going to find. After all, it's a big ocean out there.

There is, of course, a greed factor to treasure hunting, but according to Clifton, a treasure is only worth what someone is willing to pay for it.

While in Fenwick, you may want to get something to eat at **Catch 54** or **Papa Grande's.**

The other shipwreck museum, the **Treasures of the Sea Exhibit**, is located inside the library on the campus of Delaware Technical Community College on DE 404 outside **Georgetown**. This unobtrusive exhibit is also worth a visit for adults and children fascinated by treasure and the hunt for riches.

The exhibit is a collection of Spanish treasure from a 17th-century shipwreck, the *Atocha,* which went down during a 1622 hurricane off the Florida coast. On display are actual artifacts from the ship. Although this is not a local Delaware story, the information is applicable to hundreds of shipwrecks that went down in the waters off the Delaware coast.

For instance, the gold and silver ingots, as well as the coinage, are not unlike those that would have been on ships traveling nearby, especially Spanish ones like the *Atocha.*

Shipwreck Treasure

Coins provide archaeologists with valuable clues as to the date of a shipwreck. Most coins minted prior to 1732 do not have specific dates like modern coinage. However, a royal coat of arms on an old coin helps researchers and treasure hunters determine which king was in power when the coins were minted.

Gold was taxed 20 percent in Spain. Jewelry, however, was considered personal property and thus not listed on a ship's manifest, which meant it was tax-free. Many people turned gold into extremely heavy chains to wear back to Europe to avoid paying tax. The largest chains were 6 feet long.

It's important to know what was in the ships' cargoes to get a sense of what you're hoping to find.

Pieces of eight (Spanish reales) were made of silver. Doubloons were made of gold.

Gold was considered a nobleman's currency, whereas common workers were paid in copper coins. Both gold and copper from various shipwrecks have turned up on the Delaware coastline.

Rough-cut Colombian emeralds were among the valuables on many ships headed back to Europe.

The exhibit is open for limited hours, so check ahead. There's a small admission fee, but it's a good place to spend an hour, especially during cloudy or rainy weather.

Many visitors hesitate to walk into the vault in back because it looks as if it's off-limits, but if it's open, be sure to go in. Some of the most impressive treasures—gorgeous gold and emeralds—are inside.

Tricky, turbulent weather that includes hurricanes and nor'easters, strong winds, and heavy fog are dangers to maritime travel. Add in pirates, uncharted waters, and until the last century, a lack of modern communication and navigational tools, and this combination made the shallow waters of the Delaware Bay, with its rocks and shoals, dangerous and frequently deadly. Equally perilous or perhaps more perilous was the Atlantic Ocean.

Journeys to Philadelphia were treacherous; as a consequence, many shipwrecks litter the bottom of the Atlantic Ocean and Delaware Bay. Artifacts and treasure have been recovered, but so much more is yet to be found. Lost treasure lies buried beneath the region's waters.

If you're on the Atlantic beaches, especially after a storm, that may be your best chance of finding treasures in the sand. When the ocean churns and the sky grows dark and menacing, wait until the next day after the sunshine returns to look for remnants of the disturbance on shore. Driftwood, sea glass (if you're lucky), seashells, and Spanish or other old coins (if you're really lucky) are all possible finds.

Riverbanks and bay beaches are also sources of treasure after a storm. However, many of these waterfronts are on private property, so avoid trespassing. Make sure to find public property on which to do a search.

No one wants to give away their secret spots, especially if they've been lucky enough to find treasures in a special location. Some experts take a kayak out to places where sea glass is prevalent, for instance. Some advise you to go out at 7 a.m. on a February morning after a storm for your best chance of finding sea glass. For those who like to sleep in, especially on cold mornings, perhaps it's best to give the search over to quixotic chance.

Actually, sea glass is hard to spot on a beach with shells and stones, so buying a few pieces might be easier, though less challenging. Alternatively, try searching during low tide, when an extra stretch of sandy shoreline is exposed, to maximize your chances.

If it's sea glass you're after, there's a store in Lewes that sells jewelry made from sea glass—**Sand N Stones** on Front Street. There's also a store in St. Michaels that sells loose sea glass as well as jewelry and other items made from the time- and water-worn glass—**Ophiuroidea**, or "O" for short, on Talbot Street.

If it's Cape May diamonds you're after, you can easily find them at Sunset Beach, New Jersey, on Cape May Point. Sometimes they wash ashore in Delaware too, but then they're considered Delaware diamonds, though they are the same opaque stones—time- and water-polished pieces of quartz.

History of Coin Beach. **Coin Beach** is on a stretch of Atlantic Ocean coastline in Delaware, actually part of **Delaware Seashore State Park** north of the Indian River Inlet and alongside the **Indian River Life-Saving Station**. The inlet connects the ocean and Indian River Bay.

Access to Coin Beach is restricted from the lifesaving station. To get to the beach, treasure hunters need to access the beach a mile or so north or south of the area and hike to where the lifesaving station is visible.

Coin Beach is an area where remains of pirate and other ship treasures have been found in the past. One particular Irish immigrant ship, the *Faithful Steward,* sank offshore here in 1785, and the beach in front of the wreck is now unofficially dubbed Coin Beach. Many foreign coins, especially pennies with the British king's face on them, have turned up from this wreck. If you're extremely lucky, you might find some. Although salt water corrodes metal, these coins are still highly desirable.

The first coins were found on this stretch of beach in 1878, when two gold pieces and a Spanish coin were discovered by a lucky tourist. The nickname Coin Beach was first used in 1937 after many 18th-century English pennies and halfpennies washed up on the shore.

COIN BEACH

Subsequent treasure hunters have found Spanish and French coins, but most have been British, frequently from the reigns of George II and George III in the 18th and early 19th centuries.

How did these coins get here? Most likely many of the coins date back to the ship *Three Brothers*, which ran aground on a sandbar in 1775 with a cargo of copper, silver, and gold coins. The ship was on its way to the colony of Pennsylvania to pay British soldiers. At that time, there was a coin shortage in the colonies.

Another ship, the French *Count Durant,* was wrecked in 1783. This one included a cargo of French silver crowns, Spanish pieces of eight, and English copper coins.

Experts surmise that most of the coins originated on the *Faithful Steward*. The ship departed from Ireland and sank during the 1785 storm when it hit the shoals (a sandbar or sandbank beneath the water that presents a navigational hazard). On board were about 400 barrels of British pennies and halfpennies that fell into the sea when the ship went down.

Contributing to the ship's demise was a party the night before, during which the captain and crew became inebriated.

Although the ship was only 100 to 150 yards from shore, hurricane-high waves and punishing winds made swimming to shore impossible for many of the men, women, and children on board. Some did manage to swim to safety, however.

BRASS POWDER CO
PRE 1915 Used to store blac
bags for firing the
made of brass bec
not produce

Audio Tour
Irish Pennies
11

SHIPWRECK COINS
c 1785 Found on the beach near
Indian River Life-Saving Station.
*Donated by the Williams family
of Bethany Beach.*

SHIPWRECK COINS DISPLAYED AT THE LIFESAVING STATION NEXT TO COIN BEACH

Storms frequently hammer the coast, including hurricanes and nor'easters. After a storm, treasure seekers are often seen on Coin Beach, many with metal detectors. If coins are discovered, the finders consider themselves lucky, even though those finds are the result of tragedy and maritime disaster.

Pirate treasure is another possible find along the Delaware coast. As late as 1698, pirates, including the infamous Captain Kidd, visited Lewes. Kidd also reportedly buried treasure in the sand dunes near Cape May Point, New Jersey, and rumor has it that Blackbeard visited Cape May as well.

Pirates plundered ships in the Delaware Bay and used the area's inlets, barrier islands, and creeks to elude detection and capture. No one knows where some of that treasure may suddenly reappear one day.

Shopping. Delaware has no sales tax. That's the case throughout the state, so you automatically save several percent on your purchases if you're from a nearby state. Couple that with outlet shopping, and the deals get even better. If you go to the three **Tanger Outlets** on DE 1 in Rehoboth Beach, there are deals galore.

Everyone loves a bargain, especially around holidays, when we may need something special, or, more likely, when we just covet a new shiny object or outfit, even a new pair of running shoes for breaking in while dodging the tides along the shore.

Okay, so you've looked at the custom-made sea glass jewelry in Lewes,

Metal Detectors

Armed with metal detectors, modern-day treasure hunters sometimes find gold coins and other valuables on the Delaware, Maryland, and Jersey shores, especially after a storm.

One woman with a vacation condo in North Ocean City, Maryland, keeps about $10 worth of change handy, which she flings out onto the sand. As people with metal detectors walk along the beach, she watches everyone get excited when their metal detectors start to beep. Another person, who has his own metal-detecting equipment, cautions you may find things you don't want—like tin cans, for instance.

Everyone loves a treasure hunt. If you don't take it seriously and just try to have fun, you may be less disappointed if you fail to find gold cargo from a shipwreck on the shoals. Then again, you never know. Someone has to find these riches when they are spat out by the sea.

Finding metal detectors for rent appears to be as difficult as finding the treasures themselves. To buy one, you can go online or head to one of the **Bass Pro Shops** (www.basspro.com) that sell them. There's a Bass Pro Shop at the Arundel Mills mall outside Annapolis.

Prices for detectors range from about $100 to more than $1,000; the cost depends on how many bells and whistles you want. Or you can find a friend with one and borrow it. These devices literally do have bells, and determining what the sounds mean is a day's project in itself. Some detectors are even waterproof, so you can search in shallow water.

Don't overlook searching along riverbeds. After all, ships went up and down the rivers too, and there were battles all over the region, especially during the War of 1812.

Of course, be careful not to search on private property. And if you're lucky enough to discover a great find, don't announce it to the world. Think before you share, as tempting as talking may be.

Although many beaches allow the use of these devices, they are prohibited in some places. Check in advance.

And don't forget to bring a shovel of some sort. If the metal detector registers something, you'll probably have to dig 10 inches to a foot down. In the sand on a beach, that might be feasible to do by hand, but in dirt on a riverbed, you'll need some sort of shovel or trowel.

you've searched for sea glass on the beach, and you've shopped at the Tanger Outlets. Maybe you still want more. (Don't we all?)

Rehoboth Beach has lots of restaurant treasures too: places where you can find delicious and enjoyable meals. Two you might want to try are **a(MUSE)** and **Back Porch Café**.

TANGER OUTLETS IN REHOBOTH

On your way home, a stop in **St. Michaels** should be on the schedule. Take DE 404 West from the Delaware beaches to MD 404 West. Turn onto US 50 East and take a slight right onto MD 322 South, followed by a sharp left onto Easton Parkway. Then take the first right onto MD 33 West (St. Michaels Road), which becomes Talbot Street in town.

Shopping in St. Michaels is akin to shopping on a boardwalk: There are kitschy T-shirts and pillows decorated with crabs, several ice cream and cupcake shops, a high-end jeweler, and assorted other resort-style gift shops.

There's nothing terribly exciting until you happen upon a former flour mill and sewing factory. Inside there are several shops, the most notable being "O," short for **Ophiuroidea** (pronounced *o-phi-u-roy-dea*), which is a kind of starfish.

The shop has a drawer full of shells that kids can buy for a dollar a scoop. It also sells loose sea glass, as well as jewelry fashioned from sea glass and lights fashioned from empty SeaGlass wine bottles. There are many interesting items at varying prices.

Continue on to **Tilghman Island** by getting back on MD 33 West. Past the drawbridge several blocks on the left, you'll come to the **Tilghman Island Country Store**. The store carries a small selection of gift items made from sea glass. It's also a good place to buy deli sandwiches and snacks for the ride home.

With all your newly found and purchased treasures safely packed in the car, plus some food for the drive, get back on US 50 and head west to the Chesapeake Bay Bridge.

IN THE AREA

Annapolis

Attractions and Recreation

BASS PRO SHOPS. Call 410-689-2500. Website: basspro.com.

Fenwick Island, Delaware

Attractions and Recreation

DISCOVERSEA SHIPWRECK MUSEUM. Call 302-539-9366 or 1-888-743-5524. Website: www.discoversea.com.

Dining/Drinks

CATCH 54. Call 302-436-8600. Website: www.catch54.com.

PAPA GRANDE'S. Call 302-436-7272. Website: www.papagrandes.com.

Georgetown, Delaware

Attractions and Recreation

TREASURES OF THE SEA EXHIBIT. Call 302-856-5700 or 302-259-6150. Website: www.treasuresofthesea.org.

Lewes, Delaware

Accommodations

THE INN AT CANAL SQUARE. Call 302-644-3377 or 1-888-644-1911. Website: www.theinnatcanalsquare.com.

Attractions and Recreation

SAND N STONES. Call 302-270-7027. Website: www.sandnstones.com.

Rehoboth Beach, Delaware

Accommodations

BOARDWALK PLAZA HOTEL. Call 302-227-7169 or 1-800-332-3224. Website: www.boardwalkplaza.com.

Attractions and Recreation

COIN BEACH, Delaware Seashore State Park. Call 302-227-2800. Website: www.destateparks.com/Beaches/DelawareSeashore.

INDIAN RIVER LIFE-SAVING STATION. Call 302-227-6991. Website: destateparks.com/History/IRLifesavingStation.

TANGER OUTLETS, in Midway, Seaside, and Bayside. Call 302-226-9223 or 1-866-665-8682. Website: www.tangeroutlet.com/rehoboth.

Dining/Drinks

A(MUSE.). Call 302-227-7107. Website: www.amuse-rehoboth.com.

BACK PORCH CAFÉ. Call 302-227-3674. Website: www.backporchcafe .com.

St. Michaels, Maryland

Attractions and Recreation

OPHIUROIDEA. Call 410-745-8057. Website: www.ophiuroidea.com.

Tilghman Island, Maryland

Attractions and Recreation

TILGHMAN ISLAND COUNTRY STORE. Call 410-886-2777. Website: tilghmanisland.com/bars-restaurants/tilghman-island-country-store.

15

SEARCHING LABYRINTHS, HISTORIC CEMETERIES, AND MASON-DIXON MARKERS

ESTIMATED LENGTH: 350 miles round-trip

ESTIMATED TIME: 3 days

GETTING THERE: Starting from the Chesapeake Bay Bridge, travel on US 50 East, staying to the right to get on Ocean Gateway. Pass Easton and drive another 5 miles. Turn left onto Manadier Road and park your car.

HIGHLIGHTS: Mason-Dixon Line markers, Transpeninsular Line markers, labyrinths styled after the famous one at Chartres in France, historic churches and cemeteries, ghost stories and haunted places.

Certain places act as conduits to the spiritual world. Often, but not always, these are religious sites or places where the dead are hidden or buried.

Historic cemeteries offer a glimpse into the past while also providing religious and spiritual vibrations for some people who are tuned in to such energy. Some find cemeteries peaceful, interesting places. Others find them creepy. It often depends on the cemetery, the setting, and who is buried there. This is not about visiting a dead relative or friend; it's about seeking out historical figures, whether famous or forgotten.

Outside **Easton**, there's a self-directed **Cemetery Quest** tour that rambles through the countryside for 28 miles. Designed as a bike tour, it can also be done by car. Many old cemeteries are on the route, and it is fascinating to find "Goldie, spaniel" buried next to her owners in a human cemetery dating back to the 1800s.

A map of this and other bicycle tours is available from the Talbot County Office of Tourism on South Harrison Street in Easton. You can find it online at tourtalbot.org/wp-content/uploads/2014/09/TCOT-Bike-Trails.pdf.

MASON-DIXON MILE MARKER NEAR GOLDSBORO

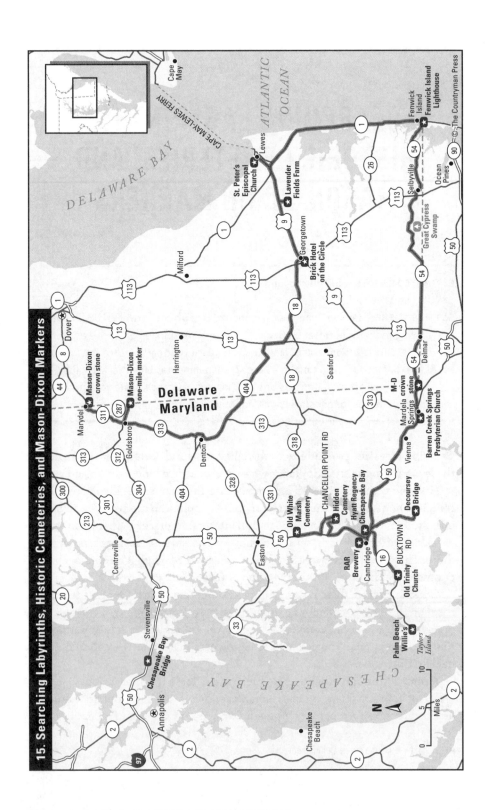

©The Countryman Press

Cape May

ATLANTIC OCEAN

DELAWARE BAY

CAPE MAY–LEWES FERRY

Lewes

St. Peter's Episcopal Church

Lavender Fields Farm

Georgetown

Brick Hotel on the Circle

Fenwick Island

Fenwick Island Lighthouse

Selbyville

Ocean Pines

Great Cypress Swamp

Milford

Dover

Harrington

Mason-Dixon crown stone

Mason-Dixon one-mile marker

Marydel

Goldsboro

Seaford

Delaware
Maryland

Denton

M-D stone

Mardela Springs

Barren Creek Springs Presbyterian Church

Vienna

Delmar

CHANCELLOR POINT RD

Old White Marsh Cemetery

Hidden Cemetery

Hyatt Regency Chesapeake Bay

Decoursey Bridge

BUCKTOWN RD

RAR Brewery

Cambridge

Old Trinity Church

Palm Beach Willie's

Taylors Island

Easton

Centreville

Stevensville

Chesapeake Bay Bridge

Annapolis

Chesapeake Beach

CHESAPEAKE BAY

N

Miles
0 5 10

Also on the cemetery tour are remnants of a brick church, with Robert Morris Sr. buried beside it in **Old White Marsh Cemetery**. His son Robert Morris Jr. helped finance the American Revolution and helped found the delightful town of Oxford on the Tred Avon River. The cemetery is at the intersection of US 50 (Ocean Gateway) and Manadier Road, which is where you parked to start this trip.

Walk around the cemetery and find Morris's marker next to the remains of the church.

This cemetery also features prominently in a haunting, centuries-old tale. Grave robbers allegedly broke into the casket of the local preacher's wife to steal the jewelry with which she'd been buried. The robbers were unable to dislodge a coveted ruby ring from her finger, so they began to cut the finger off.

As if in a tale by Edgar Allan Poe, the woman awoke. Apparently, she'd been in a coma, not dead, an error that used to happen more often than is comfortable to contemplate. One robber ran off, while the other fell into the grave, hitting his head and rendering himself lifeless. The woman, her finger bleeding and disfigured, climbed out and walked home, where she lived to be an old woman. Or that's how the story goes.

Also on the cemetery tour is **Hidden Cemetery**, set back about 20 feet from a road in the woods. It's located off Chancellor Point Road close to the turnoff for Money Maker Road. Follow the bike map to find it, but pay close attention, as it's easier to see a deer darting about than it is to see the headstones in what appears to be this small family burial ground. Pieces of split-rail fencing hidden amid the vegetation hint at the cemetery's location, but it's difficult to spot.

Rabbits and squirrels run freely in many of these cemeteries. You might even get lucky and catch a peek of an albino squirrel seeming to read a headstone. These are country pleasures, back road adventures—relaxed and quirky reasons for getting out on isolated and somewhat deserted roadways.

You can certainly wander around on your own and stop at any cemetery you find. It's always interesting to read the dates and names, or any epitaph chosen to memorialize a particular person. You might use your imagination to guess at his or her life story from such brief, cursory data. Sometimes nearby tombstones of relatives long lost tell part of the tale, sometimes not.

The cemeteries mentioned in this itinerary are just a starting point for exploring the past in this way. Sometimes visiting cemeteries is peaceful, sometimes disturbing, but a view into the past is always challenging and perhaps intoxicating, for we all desire to be remembered after our time comes.

Next, get back on US 50 East and cross the Choptank River Bridge into

GROUNDS OF HYATT REGENCY ON THE CHOPTANK RIVER

Cambridge. There is a lovely bed-and-breakfast in Cambridge, as well as the delightful **Hyatt Regency Chesapeake Bay Golf Resort, Spa & Marina**. Cambridge is a good place to spend the night and there are several excellent restaurants. **Blackwater Bakery** is a cheerful choice for breakfast or lunch, and the seasonally-opened **Blue Point Provision Company** at the Hyatt is good for dinner.

But it's early, so continue on US 50 East until you get to MD 16 West (Church Creek Road). Take MD 16 through the town of Church Creek toward **Taylors Island**.

Go about 8 miles and stop at **Old Trinity Church** on Taylors Island Road. You're southwest of Cambridge at the cemetery where Anna Ella Carroll is buried. She was credited by some with being an unofficial member of President Abraham Lincoln's cabinet; if that's true, she was the first woman in a position with that much power.

Carroll was the daughter of Maryland governor Thomas King Carroll and a seasoned political writer. According to her stone, she lived from 1815 to 1893 (though the actual date of her death was 1894). She supposedly influenced Lincoln by helping to conceive the Union's successful Tennessee River military campaign and lending assistance to the president on the subject of his constitutional war powers.

Some feel Lincoln overstepped those powers. In that case, Carroll assisted him in putting the end, or results, ahead of the means, or methods.

The church and adjoining cemetery are on the banks of **Church Creek**, a tributary of the Little Choptank River.

The members of the Carroll family, including Anna, were slave owners. However, Anna was committed to the gradual ending of slavery.

Tales of life and death. Taking a walk is always a delightful way to explore a place. It's also the only way to truly discover the fascinating tales of life and death that reside in cemeteries.

Burial customs have varied over the years, based on differences in religions and eras. As mentioned earlier, in some cases you can find pets buried with their owners. There are also cenotaphs—markers without graves that honor people buried elsewhere.

Whether from the inscriptions on the stones, the stories of locals, or the whispers of the spirits, one gets the sense less of an eerie epic than of a light-hearted look at people who are long gone but are still lingering in memory, in resident ghosts, and in the churches and houses left behind.

If looking for spirits makes you hungry, you can have lunch at **Palm Beach Willie's** about 8 miles farther west on Taylors Island Road (16 miles from US 50 in Cambridge). Or you can grab a sandwich and some ice cream at **Emily's Produce** on Church Creek Road; it's open mid-April through Thanksgiving.

After lunch, head to **Decoursey Bridge** near **Vienna**, Maryland, where the famous ghost story of Big Liz still scares residents and visitors alike.

To get there, drive back on MD 16 East, then make a right on US 50 East. Travel about half a mile and make a right on Bucktown Road. Take Bucktown Road to Decoursey Bridge Road, where you'll turn left. If you reach a three-way intersection, you've gone too far.

Once on Decoursey Bridge Road, continue until you reach the small bridge across the **Transquaking River**.

According to local legend, Big Liz was a slave during the Civil War. Her master wanted to hide his fortune, so he had Big Liz, who was nearly 8 feet tall, carry his treasure chest to the marsh and bury it.

Afterward, he cut off her head so she couldn't tell anyone where the fortune was buried. It's reported that if you park on the bridge at night, your car doors and trunk will pop open, and Big Liz will walk by, carrying her head in her arms.

In another version of the tale, Big Liz will appear, again with her head in her hands, if you park on the bridge at night, honk three times, and put your keys on top of the car. Teenagers from the area are scared silly when they do this, usually after a party.

Even as adults, many of them won't go back except in the daytime; it's an isolated spot and really lends itself to this spooky tale. Mention Big Liz to anyone within a 50-mile radius and you'll likely evoke a smile (and maybe a shiver).

Head back into Cambridge. If you want a drink, go to **RAR Brewing**, a local brewery that has a Decoursey Bridge street sign on the wall. At one point, the brewery sold Big Lizz Harvest Ale seasonally in October, no doubt to play up the story of Big Liz for the Halloween season. Though they've retired this seasonal butternut squash beer, everyone always asks for it, so it's possible it may be brought back.

With regard to the Decoursey Bridge street sign, apparently the sign on the bridge itself winds up missing on a regular basis. As to the one that's been on the wall at RAR for several years, one of the managers merely shrugged, explaining, "This one just showed up."

RAR is located on Poplar Street in what was previously a pool hall and fixture of the community for 50 years.

You can't go wrong staying at the **Cambridge House Bed & Breakfast**, which is within walking distance of several good restaurants for dinner, including **Bistro Poplar, Snappers Waterfront Café**, and **Portside.**While you're in town, there are some outdoor murals that are definitely worth seeing. A talented artist can capture the spirits of those he or she depicts, whether humans or wildlife. And these murals in Cambridge seem to come

MURAL OF HARRIET TUBMAN ON THE SIDE WALL OF THE HARRIET TUBMAN MUSEUM IN DOWNTOWN CAMBRIDGE

alive from the structures upon which they are painted. One of the murals, of a great blue heron about to eat a crab, is on the side of the J.M. Clayton Co. Seafood building at 108 Commerce Street.

Another is of Underground Railroad heroine Harriet Tubman extending a hand on the side wall of the small Harriet Tubman Museum at 424 Race Street (not to be confused with the much larger Underground Railroad Visitor Center in the midst of Blackwater National Wildlife Refuge). This mural of Tubman has gained worldwide attention.

If you stay at the Hyatt Regency Chesapeake Bay Golf Resort, Spa & Marina, the entrance is directly across the street from MD 16, where it forms a T with US 50; there are several restaurants within the resort too.

In the morning, have breakfast and then head out in search of **Mason-Dixon Line markers** and other markers. They look like headstones, but they're not.

The carved Mason-Dixon (M-D) markers were shipped to the American colonies from Great Britain. Made of limestone quarried in Britain, the stones were carefully placed by astronomer Charles Mason and surveyor Jeremiah Dixon to solve a border dispute between the Penns to the north (Pennsylvania) and the Calverts to the south (Maryland).

Both Mason and Dixon were English, and they came to America in 1763 at the behest of the British king after William Penn petitioned the crown to settle the dispute. Divisions of land were often about taxes and power, so the disputed territory was vitally important.

At the time, there was no United States yet; there were just colonies. And the three counties that now comprise Delaware were, at the time, the three southernmost counties of Pennsylvania. Thus, the M-D markers separate Delaware from Maryland as well as Maryland from Pennsylvania.

Mason and Dixon took five years to mark the property lines by using the stars. In the end, they marked a 233-mile boundary between Pennsylvania and Maryland, and an 83-mile path going north and south between what is now Maryland and Delaware.

One-mile markers have a *P* on one side and an *M* on the other. Every 5 miles, a special stone was placed with the Penn and Calvert coats of arms on opposite sides; these special stones are called crown stones.

Many of the stones are gone as a result of weather damage, farm accidents with tractors and other equipment, theft, and vandalism. Several of the remaining stones are encased in metal cage-like structures for their own protection and to preserve history.

The **M-D crown stone** in **Delmar** is so encased, in the southwest corner of Delaware. It's placed there with three other stones—one is the midpoint **Transpeninsular Line marker**, which marks the southern boundary of Delaware as well as the midpoint of the Delmarva Peninsula (halfway between the Atlantic Ocean and the Chesapeake Bay). The other two are smaller markers put there by local surveyors before Mason and Dixon placed the crown stone.

To see the crown stone in Delmar, travel on US 50 East (the lifeline highway of the Eastern Shore) to the light at **Mardela Springs**. You'll come back here, but for now turn left onto Delmar Road and drive about 3 miles. On your left, you'll see a small curved drive in front of what looks like a metal cage with a roof on top. Pull into the curved drive and take a look at the markers inside the cage-like structure.

Now everyone is friendly, and it matters little what state you're in, except for property and income taxes, school districts, and political representation. But the borders are interesting, for the history that led up to the formation of the United States matters.

Many people are under the mistaken belief that the Mason-Dixon Line originated during the Civil War and it separated north from south; that is only partially true. The line did come to symbolize the separation of the Union states from the Confederate states. However, the line is on the northern border of Maryland, and though its leaders were conflicted, Maryland stayed with the Union.

From Delmar, a town that straddles Delaware and Maryland, drive back along Delmar Road and go through the light at the intersection with US 50. After you cross US 50, you're in the town of Mardela Springs. Go past a few

GREAT CYPRESS SWAMP

houses on the left and turn up the gravel drive into the parking lot of **Barren Creek Springs Presbyterian Church**.

Among the handful of tombstones is a spare M-D marker, just sitting in the graveyard. It doesn't actually mark the Mason-Dixon Line, but it's intriguing that this stone ended up here in a churchyard a few miles away from the line. Not many people know it's here, or at least they didn't before now.

The local story is that the people bringing the stones to the appropriate places determined by Mason and Dixon went up the wrong creek. There may have been two or three of the stones on the boat, and those stones were heavy (300 to 600 pounds each). To lighten the load, the people transporting the stones may have left one of them along the shore. It would have been easy for them to say the boat turned over and one stone was lost.

Of course, this is probably speculation. Or perhaps it's the truth, passed down through the generations.

In the early 1800s, the town of Mardela Springs was a spa resort where visitors came to "take the waters." The grand hotel burned to the ground in 1914, and the mineral springs, though it still exists, is a mere shadow of its former self—merely a trickle in the springhouse, which is still there, just past the church on Main Street.

The history of the town, coupled with the M-D marker, makes for a colorful visit.

If you want to go to Mardela Springs before seeing the crown stone in Delmar, and you're heading east from Cambridge along US 50, after you cross over the Nanticoke River Bridge, you'll soon see a sign that directs you to Mardela Springs by veering off on a road to the right. If you take that road, you're on "old US 50," which is also Main Street.

Drive through town, with its mixture of various architectural styles. You'll loop around, and just before the light at US 50, you'll see the gravel drive leading up to the church with the tiny cemetery next to it. That's where the spare M-D marker is kept.

There's a creek behind the church where the Nanticoke Indians reportedly spent time. There's even a marker in the cemetery honoring the Native Americans supposedly buried there. The church and cemetery are on a bit of a hill, so it was quite possibly sacred ground to the Nanticokes, who would have wanted higher ground to bury the dead without fear of the graves flooding.

Locals say a few tomahawks were found a long time ago by people from town who were fishing in the creek.

Before it was known as Mardela Springs, the town was called Barren Creek, thus the name on the church.

While you're in town and before reaching the light at US 50, you can turn onto Bratten Street and go to Railroad Avenue. There you'll see some old structures, including a railroad depot.

If you want to go to Salisbury, the largest city on Maryland's Eastern Shore, it's only about 15 minutes away. Ocean City is only about 30 minutes east, and the bay is only about 30 minutes south.

The role of Taylors Island. Before you leave this part of Maryland, you should know that Taylors Island, where you were near Old Trinity Church, played a part in the Mason-Dixon Line. That may seem counterintuitive since the Chesapeake Bay is nowhere near the Pennsylvania or Delaware borders.

But land is valuable today, and it was valuable back then too. Every bit of advantage was apparently utilized, and a controversy broke out over whether Taylors Island was actually an island or not.

If it was part of the mainland, its westernmost point would be considered the edge of the Transpeninsular Line, thus resulting in Maryland losing some acreage.

If the island was determined to be an actual island, the Transpeninsular Line would end before the island started, and Maryland's half would extend farther into the peninsula, giving Maryland more acreage.

It was decided that Taylors Island was indeed an island, so Maryland won that battle.

But for this trip, you're going to head back into Delaware on Delmar Road, past the crown stone, and into the town of Delmar, several miles farther on DE 54. The town of Delmar is half in Maryland and half in Delaware, thus

ST. PETER'S LABYRINTH IN LEWES

the name. When you cross the railroad tracks, you'll see a teeny tiny park next to it. Turn left and stop for a bit to visit this miniature outdoor railroad museum.

From Delmar, you'll be heading to **Fenwick Island**, where another Transpeninsular Line marker is located in front of **Fenwick Island Lighthouse**. Fenwick Island is in Delaware just north of Ocean City, Maryland.

You can follow MD 54 and DE 54 to Fenwick. On the way, you'll pass **Selbyville**, a Delaware town on the edge of the **Great Cypress Swamp**.

The swamp has a local monster legend, not dissimilar to the legends of Bigfoot and other monsters. Supposedly, the swamp monster is a big brown blur known to jump out at cars along the road at night.

Half the fun of driving or hiking the swamp is getting lost—for those who like that sort of thing. Nighttime can be particularly creepy, with the dark, unlighted dirt road winding through stands of trees. The forest is wetland and it can easily become flooded, so choose your night carefully.

Due to its location on the border between Maryland and Delaware, there are not many police patrols in the Great Cypress Swamp. Thus, deer hunters and wild turkey hunters abound, as well as ne'er-do-wells looking to drink and stir up trouble in the swamp.

The swamp extends from Selbyville in Delaware to **Pocomoke City** in southeastern Maryland. It is also known as the Burnt Swamp, for several fires have decimated large portions of the woodlands, sometimes burning for months underground, just under the surface of the quicksand-like, peatrich soil.

The cypress stands once covered 50,000 acres. Now there are just 10,000 acres of woodlands, though that is still substantial.

Slave labor was used to dredge the swamp before the Civil War and prior to emancipation. At Shepherd's Crossing in Maryland, Prohibition stills were once prevalent, which likely was the cause of at least some of the fires.

After you pass Selbyville, you'll arrive in Fenwick Island, where the lighthouse is an iconic landmark. Beneath the lighthouse is a Transpeninsular Line marker. Transpeninsular markers were placed on the southern boundary of what were then the three southernmost counties of Pennsylvania and is now Delaware. These markers were not placed by Mason and Dixon but by others.

From Fenwick, get on DE 1 North (Coastal Highway) to Lewes (pronounced *lew-is*). Once in Lewes, turn right onto Savannah Road and then left onto Second Street into the heart of the little town.

In the center of Lewes, the cemetery at **St. Peter's Episcopal Church** is in the front yard of the church. Founded in 1681, St. Peter's claim to fame is that it's "the first church in the first town in the first state."

This is an unusual cemetery, with historic figures, victims of nearby

Meditative Paths

Labyrinths are ancient symbols that belong to various traditions. A labyrinth is not to be confused with a maze, which has tricks and dead ends, nor is a labyrinth a puzzle that needs to be solved.

Instead, a labyrinth has only one path. As a metaphor for a spiritual journey, walking the winding path of a labyrinth is contemplative and meant to put people in touch with their inner selves.

A labyrinth is useful as a stress reliever or to assist people in making decisions or healing (whether literally or figuratively).

There is no right or wrong way to walk the path and no set speed. If you concentrate and follow the winding path, you will arrive at the center, where you can pause if you like. Whenever you're ready, you can walk back out the same way you came in, again going at whatever speed you like.

shipwrecks, and people of various religions buried there because it was the only cemetery in town for so long.

Adjacent to the cemetery and open to the public is a path of peace, reminiscent of a labyrinth. It's not a fancy path, but it's circular and meditative, and it's in a lovely town.

The interesting thing about historic cemeteries like this one is the people buried there and the stories that surround them. Of course, there is the inevitable mistake or unusual bit of information on the tombstones. A pertinent date carved into one stone at St. Peter's is February 30—except there never is or was a February 30. February 29 occurs once every four years, but then it's March 1. Oops . . . a mistake for eternity?

There are many great restaurants in Lewes where you can have an enjoyable meal. **Agave Mexican Restaurant & Tequila Bar**, **Half Full** (pizza), and **Striper Bites Bistro** (seafood) are a few good choices.

Back on the road, head to **Lavender Fields Farm**, which is a lovely spot to walk a labyrinth. To get there, take DE 1, which runs north and south in Delaware. From DE 1 in either direction, take US 9/DE 404 West for about 4 miles toward the town of Georgetown. Just before the railroad tracks, turn left onto Cool Springs Road and drive 0.7 mile. The farm is on the right.

Owned by two women, the 5-acre farm is a place where you can wander around and enjoy the lavender plants at no charge, visit the on-site store, have a light picnic (make sure to clean up afterward), and walk the labyrinth on the grounds.

The labyrinth is a replica of the famous one at Chartres Cathedral in France. Plus, there are hundreds of lavender plants all around, which smell wonderful and act as a natural bug repellent—something useful near the shore in the summer.

Lavender is aromatic and useful for its calming and comforting properties. The labyrinth at Chartres and its replicas are also useful for relaxation and meditation. By concentrating on the path you must walk, your focus is on staying within the lines and following the intricate route, which tends to relax and disperse worries, even if only for a little while.

The lavender farm is the essence of bucolic, yet it's near the commercial corridor that is DE 1 and the Atlantic beaches, which, in the summer, are often mobbed (especially on weekends). Still, you'll find real moments of tranquility here, including at the farm's relatively new zen garden.

Ghosts, apparitions, zombies, and other spirits. Some people are charmed by those who come back as ghosts . . . or who never really left. Others can do without them. But wherever you fall on this pendulum, the ghosts are out there, waiting for recognition, waiting for you to run away or run toward them. As an added benefit, those from the spirit world inevitably come attached to a great story.

The Brick Hotel on the Circle is in the heart of the charming town of **Georgetown**, which is the Sussex County seat in the southernmost part of Delaware. There's a fountain in the middle of the circle, surrounded by a quaint town hall, a county courthouse, and many streets like spokes connected to the circle, with lots of lawyers' offices nearby.

The hotel has two ghosts, George and Ophelia, who were named by the employees. Rumor has it that Ophelia's real name is Amy, but there's no way to establish that, nor is there any way to confirm whether the hotel is really haunted.

The two alleged ghosts are friendly spirits who play little tricks in the upstairs inn, like moving items around or turning on a shower at midnight. Visitors can dine calmly downstairs, knowing that the ghosts are not likely to interfere with their excellent food and the accommodating service.

The hotel has a compelling history. It was originally a hotel that was later transformed into a bank. The wine cellar is actually housed in the former bank vault; wine is, after all, valuable. The history is mixed with modern amenities like upscale bathrooms and flat-screen TVs, creating a good balance. Located only about 12 miles from Lewes, it's in a convenient location.

Have dinner at **The Counting House Restaurant & Pub** inside The Brick Hotel and spend the night. After breakfast in the morning, get on DE 404 West, cross to MD 404, and take US 50 West to the Chesapeake Bay Bridge.

If you're still enamored with Mason-Dixon Line markers, there are two more you can see if you want to take a detour before heading home. From Georgetown, take DE 404 West to MD 313 North. At **Goldsboro**, an old railroad town, take MD 311 North. You're heading to the town of **Marydel**, which is half in Maryland and half in Delaware, just like Delmar to the south. Turn right onto Crown Stone Road (MD 454), and you'll find an M-D crown stone on your left surrounded by just a simple chain. There are apparently fewer incidents of vandalism and damage to the M-D markers in this area than along the Pennsylvania border.

In fact, there are reportedly 33 existing markers along the Maryland-Delaware border. Rumor has it that most people don't even recognize the markers as anything other than stones. Perhaps that's why they've survived.

This one in Marydel has traveled more than most. It went to the 1904 St. Louis World's Fair and later to the Maryland State House in Annapolis. At the request of Marydel citizens, it was returned in 1954 to their town.

Not far away is another, more hidden one-mile M-D marker. To get there from Marydel, return to Goldsboro on MD 311 South and turn left onto MD 287 East (Sandtown Road), which becomes DE 10 toward Sandtown. Take a right onto Bright Road, then another right onto Drapers Mill Road. Turn left onto Lords Corner Road, where you'll see a sign welcoming you to Kent County, Delaware.

Go about 200 or 300 feet farther; on your right will be the one-mile M-D marker situated between two protective pieces of metal. It's not clear what the metal is protecting against—perhaps a tree falling or a car hitting the stone. Or maybe the metal is just to help visitors find the marker, given that otherwise it's rather obscure in the dense woods.

Retrace your route back to Goldsboro and stay on MD 287 West, crossing over MD 313 North. From there, turn left onto MD 312, then right onto MD 304. From MD 304, turn left onto US 301 South, which will join up with US 50 West. Follow it across the Bay Bridge, leaving the spirits and ghosts behind.

IN THE AREA

Cambridge, Maryland

Accommodations

CAMBRIDGE HOUSE BED & BREAKFAST. Call 410-221-7700. Website: www.cambridgehousebandb.com.

HYATT REGENCY CHESAPEAKE BAY GOLF RESORT, SPA & MARINA. Call 410-901-1234. Website: www.hyatt.com/en-US/hotel/maryland/hyatt -regency-chesapeake-bay-golf-resort-spa-and-marina/chesa.

Attractions and Recreation

DECOURSEY BRIDGE, Vienna.

OLD TRINITY CHURCH, Church Creek. Call 410-228-2940. Website: www .oldtrinity.net.

PUBLIC MURALS.

Dining/Drinks

BISTRO POPLAR. Call 410-228-4884. Website: www.bistropoplar.com.

BLACKWATER BAKERY. Call 443-225-5948. Website: www.black-water -bakery.com.

BLUE POINT PROVISION COMPANY. Call 410-901-6400. Website: www .hyatt.com/en-US/hotel/maryland/hyatt-regency-chesapeake-bay-golf -resort-spa-and-marina/chesa/dining.

EMILY'S PRODUCE. Call 443-521-0789. Website: www.emilysproduce.com.

PALM BEACH WILLIE'S, Taylors Island. Call 410-221-5111. Website: www .palmbeachwilliesti.com. Closed New Year's to St. Patrick's Day.

PORTSIDE SEAFOOD RESTAURANT. Call 410-228-9007. Website: www .portsidemaryland.com.

SNAPPERS WATERFRONT CAFÉ. Call 410-228-0112. Website: www .snapperswaterfrontcafe.com.

RAR BREWING. Call 443-225-5664. Website: rarbrewing.com.

Delmar, Maryland/Delaware

Attractions and Recreation

MASON-DIXON CROWN STONE AND TRANSPENINSULAR LINE MARKER.

Easton, Maryland

Attractions and Recreation

CEMETERY QUEST (BICYCLE MAP), available from Talbot County Office of Tourism. Call 410-770-8000. Website: www.tourtalbot.org.

Fenwick Island, Delaware

Attractions and Recreation

FENWICK ISLAND LIGHTHOUSE AND TRANSPENINSULAR LINE MARKER. Website: fenwickislandlighthouse.org.

Georgetown, Delaware

Accommodations

THE BRICK HOTEL ON THE CIRCLE. Call 302-855-5800 or 1-877-882-7425. Website: www.thebrickhotel.com.

Attractions and Recreation

LAVENDER FIELDS FARM, Milton. Call 302-684-1514. Website: www .lavenderfieldsde.com.

Dining/Drinks

THE COUNTING HOUSE, inside The Brick Hotel. Call 302-856-1836. Website: thecountinghouse.net.

Lewes, Delaware

Attractions and Recreation

ST. PETER'S EPISCOPAL CHURCH. Call 302-645-8479. Website: www.st peterslewes.org.

Dining/Drinks

AGAVE MEXICAN RESTAURANT & TEQUILA BAR. Call 302-645-1232. Website: agavelewes.com.

HALF FULL. Call 302-645-8877. Website: www.halffulllewes.com.

STRIPER BITES. Call 302-645-4657. Website: www.striperbites.com.

Mardela Springs, Maryland

Attractions and Recreation

BARREN CREEK SPRINGS PRESBYTERIAN CHURCH (MASON-DIXON MILE MARKER IN THE CEMETERY).

16

KEEPING UP WITH OWLS, EAGLES, ORIOLES, AND RAVENS

ESTIMATED LENGTH: 140 miles round-trip

ESTIMATED TIME: A few day trips or overnight

GETTING THERE: Start out at the Inner Harbor in downtown Baltimore and head north on the Charles Street (MD 139) corridor.

HIGHLIGHTS: Fell's Point neighborhood, tour of iconic Bromo Seltzer Arts Tower, sightings of bald eagles at Conowingo Dam, Owl Bar Prohibition–era speakeasy, grave of Edgar Allan Poe, Ravens football, Orioles baseball, restaurants with superb crabcakes.

It's hard to comprehend the Chesapeake Bay region without a look at **Baltimore**. A major US seaport now and throughout the nation's history, the Baltimore harbor is actually on the **Patapsco River** as it empties into the bay, despite the common misconception that Baltimore is on the bay itself.

The Patapsco is one of many freshwater rivers that flow into and feed the Chesapeake. *Patapsco* is an Algonquian (Native American) name meaning "tide covered with froth" or "backwater."

One should never discount Baltimore, for much of the commerce from the Chesapeake did and does start or end in the city. Baltimore is pronounced *Bawl-mer* or *Ball-da-more* if you're a local. Maryland is often pronounced *Merlin* too. An entire book could easily be written about Baltimore, for it's replete with history and a collection of quirky neighborhoods off the beaten path even though they're within the city.

Baltimore is definitely worth visiting, if only for a day trip. The problem is choosing what to see, for one can spend a lifetime getting to know the place and its environs.

BALTIMORE HARBOR

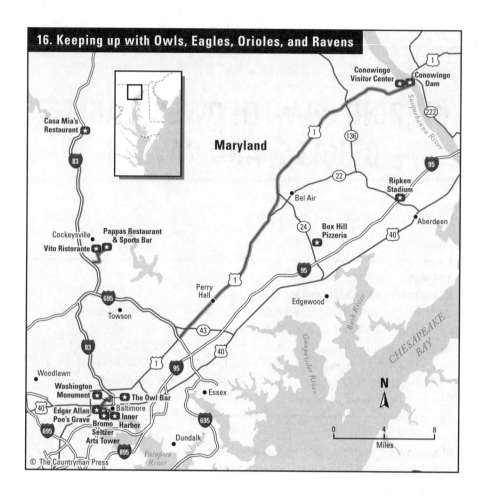

For a brief but poignant look, make sure to see some of the quirkier sites, including the **Bromo Seltzer Arts Tower**, the **Owl Bar,** and the **grave of Edgar Allan Poe**. If you are an art and history lover, a brief detour to the **Walters Art Museum** might be necessary, with its world-class exhibits from ancient Egypt, Greece, Rome, and the Near East.

The Walters is on North Charles Street in **Mt. Vernon**. While you're in that neighborhood, walk or drive by Baltimore's **Washington Monument**. Mt. Vernon is one of the neighborhoods worth exploring; others include **Fell's Point**, **Canton**, and **Hampden**.

Bromo Seltzer Arts Tower. Curiosity is a huge factor when traveling. Whether it's the Eiffel Tower in Paris, the Statue of Liberty in New York City, the Gateway Arch in St. Louis, the Golden Gate Bridge in San Francisco, or the Washington Monument in DC, these are iconic symbols.

Touring them (or crossing them, in the case of bridges like the Golden

Gate or Chesapeake Bay Bridge-Tunnel) is a challenge, and the need to do so at least once is great for satisfying your curiosity. You will likely always remember the experience.

Baltimore is no different, though its iconic symbol is less well known. Yet in its own way, that makes it more special. For not many people have toured the Bromo Seltzer Arts Tower, located within a few blocks of Camden Yards, the charming retro-style ballpark where the Orioles play.

Part of the reason few have toured the Bromo Seltzer Arts Tower is because tours only started in the summer of 2015, and you can only tour the structure on Saturdays. That's pretty limiting. But if you're in the area on a Saturday, this tour is worth an hour or so of your time.

The tower is located at the corner of South Eutaw and West Lombard Streets—easily walkable from the Inner Harbor. During the tour, you'll learn about the history of the tower, which was

ICONIC BROMO SELTZER ARTS TOWER IN DOWNTOWN BALTIMORE

designed as part of the Emerson Drug Company's headquarters. Emerson manufactured the headache remedy Bromo Seltzer.

Now an excellent example of reuse, the building currently houses artists' studios. Chief among the tour's highlights is a visit to the clock room at the top of the 15-story building. The tower has four clock faces with the letters B-R-O-M-O S-E-L-T-Z-E-R. The building originally had a rotating glowing blue bottle of Bromo Seltzer at the top, but it was removed from the tower in 1936 due to structural concerns.

Places to stay. There are lots of hotels in the city, including many around the Inner Harbor. Several blocks north of the harbor is **Kimpton Hotel Monaco Baltimore** in the unique and iconic former Baltimore & Ohio (B&O) Railroad headquarters building at North Charles and East Baltimore Streets.

The Hotel Monaco building was constructed in 1906 to replace the previous B&O headquarters, destroyed in the Great Baltimore Fire of 1904. Sculptures over the Charles Street entrance depict the Roman mythological god Mercury as a symbol of commerce, and a figure with a torch and locomotive representing the progress of industry.

WORKINGS OF BROMO SELTZER CLOCK

Hotel Monaco is on the top several floors. The rest of the building houses offices and a restaurant on the first floor.

For a quirky place to stay in a historic neighborhood, choose the **Admiral Fell Inn**. It's right at the waterfront of Fell's Point. The neighborhood was Baltimore's original deep-water port, founded in the early 1700s by two brothers from England—shopkeeper Edward Fell and shipbuilder William Fell. The area has several British street names, including Thames, Lancaster, Fleet, and Shakespeare.

Fell's Point was a point of entry for immigrants from Europe in the 18th and 19th centuries. By 1900, Fell's Point was a rough area, with its waterfront filled with saloons, brothels, and warehouses. The hotel was originally opened as a boarding house for sailors to provide a safe place for them to stay, thus enabling them to avoid being shanghaied.

Over the years, the building had various uses and fell into disrepair. Then it was renovated in 1985 and opened as an inn. The rooms are quirky, but that's part of its charm.

Ravens and Edgar Allan Poe. From downtown Baltimore, take Charles Street north to left on Fayette Street. Follow that to Greene Street and you'll see **Westminster Burying Ground**, which is where Edgar Allan Poe is buried just inside the front gate. The grave, church, and cemetery belong to the **University of Maryland Law School** next door.

When the NFL Colts sneaked out of town in the middle of a snowy night in 1984 on their way to Indianapolis, little did football fans in Baltimore realize that a dozen years later in 1996, their new NFL team, the Ravens, would be named after a poem. It's not just any poem, it's one by poet and master storyteller Edgar Allan Poe. In fact, the team's mascot is named none other than "Poe," and of course he's depicted as a giant raven.

There's certainly an avian theme that can be discerned in the city, especially if you're a sports fan. And truth is as strange as fiction when it comes to Poe. After all, like one of the characters in his stories, Poe was buried three times. First he was interred in the wrong grave in back of the cemetery, and then he was moved to the correct plot, also in back.

When schoolchildren saved their pennies to purchase a special stone, he was moved to the front of Westminster's graveyard. To add insult to injury, Poe's birthday is wrong on the new "penny" marker; it's off by one day.

Several other cities claim Poe, for he lived in Richmond, Philadelphia, and Boston at various times. But with Poe's grave here, and because he did live in Baltimore at one time, the city claims him as their own. Fans come from around the world to pay homage to Poe at this cemetery, which is old enough to have once been called a graveyard. There is a kind of "poetic" justice that his burial site is an internationally recognized place of interest.

Tales of terror come to mind in the presence of the man's remains, for Poe is considered "the father of the modern detective story." After all, he created C. Auguste Dupin—the first fictional detective ever—in his short story, "The Murders in the Rue Morgue."

Poe's own sad story fascinates his fans. His was a short but prolific life. He delved into the mysteries of the mind, transporting others on his journeys into the dark, the tragic, the beautiful, and the moving. These are perfect topics for a cool, clear night on the streets of a Baltimore filled with much history and many ghosts.

The Ravens play at **M&T Stadium** downtown, where, if you're lucky, you'll be able to obtain tickets to catch a game. The team's colors are purple and black; and fans all over the area are likely to wear the popular color combination during football season.

Washington Monument (not the one in Washington, DC). The Baltimore monument to our first president was designed by Robert Mills, the same architect who imagined the monument to George Washington in the nation's capital. Baltimore's monument came first, and when it was built, Baltimore was the third largest city in North America.

Construction began in 1815 and the masonry work was finished in 1829. In Washington, construction on Mill's Washington Monument began in 1848 but was incomplete until 1885. Thus, the Baltimore monument was particularly important.

The monument stands at 178 feet 8 inches high in Mt. Vernon Square, perhaps a bit ironic because George Washington lived at another Mount Vernon—his estate along the Potomac River in Virginia. The monument's design is that of a Doric column. You can drive to the Baltimore site by taking Charles Street north from the Inner Harbor. It's about two blocks past Walters Art Museum.

Prohibition-era speakeasy. The Owl Bar is in the former Belvedere Hotel (now a condominium) at the corner of Charles and Chase Streets. To get there from downtown, just follow Charles Street North to Chase Street. Officially opened in December 1903, the bar existed years before alcohol was prohibited throughout the country. But Prohibition didn't deter the establishment's proprietors; it just cemented the bar's place in more scandalous history when it became a speakeasy.

Travelers who were in-the-know would travel by train to Baltimore's nearby Pennsylvania Station a few blocks away and stay for a few days at the Belvedere Hotel so they could imbibe illegal booze at the bar. An owl above the bar had eyes that would blink when the feds were not around. When the owl's eyes were staring straight ahead, patrons knew not to say anything.

Now, of course, you can legally enjoy alcohol, so this is a worthwhile place to have a meal and reminisce about a time gone but certainly remembered.

BALTIMORE'S WASHINGTON MONUMENT
MARY HELEN SEAY GRASSO

Orioles and IronBirds. The Orioles stadium in downtown Baltimore is on the site of a former B&O railroad yard. **Oriole Park at Camden Yards** is a delightful re-creation and modern version of an old-time ballpark.

Ripken Stadium is about an hour north of the city in Aberdeen. It's where the IronBirds, a minor league affiliate of the Orioles, play. It's a cheerful minor league stadium named for Cal Ripken Jr., former shortstop and third baseman for the Baltimore Orioles.

If it's summer, Orioles fans will be donning the team's orange and black colors. One of the city's nicknames is Birdland after the city's baseball team, the "O's," which is short for "Orioles."

Both venues—major and minor league—are worth visiting to catch a game.

Great places to dine. Besides the Owl Bar, there are many great places to eat in Baltimore City; among them are **Tio Pepe's** for Spanish cuisine (the paella is amazing) and **Aldo's** for excellent Italian fare in the city's Little Italy neighborhood.

If you want to take a drive outside the city, there are excellent spots for Maryland crabcakes. **Pappas** in Cockeysville is well known for their excellent ones and **Casa Mia's** in Parkton has crabcakes that are absolutely fantastic. Parkton is a long drive; but the crabcakes are well worth it, especially on a pretty summer night. Casa Mia's is a former biker bar that still has a lively bar along with family dining.

There's also a great Italian restaurant in the suburbs—**Vito Ristorante** in Cockeysville. Vito's is charming and intimate with fabulous pasta and seafood.

Seeing majestic bald eagles. A visit to **Conowingo Dam** is a great way to spot and photograph bald eagles. The dam was built to partially tame the **Susquehanna River**, the bay's largest tributary, for hydroelectric power.

Like the Patapsco River, the Susquehanna is a feeder river to the bay and it's a long river at 444 miles. (An Algonquian name, *Susquehanna* means "muddy current" or "winding current.") The river starts in upstate New York and ends where it meets the waters of the Chesapeake Bay in the city of Havre de Grace.

In order to view the eagles, get up super early one morning and head out of the city to Conowingo Dam. This is best done in the late fall and early winter so you can catch sight of the bald eagles soaring overhead and then diving for, and dining on, abundant fish off the dam from the Susquehanna River.

Near the river's edge, you'll find professional and amateur photographers with long lenses wearing hunters' clothing for warmth. Hopefully you'll see many bald eagles feeding too. The largest number of eagles is usually spotted from the end of October to early January.

Driving from Baltimore City, take I-83 North to I-695 East (Baltimore Beltway). From the Beltway, take exit 32B onto Belair Road (US 1 North). Eventually US 1 will change names and become Conowingo Road, leading you right to the dam.

To join the photographers and other eagle watchers, don't actually cross the dam but instead turn right just before the dam onto Shuresville Road. Then turn left on Shures Landing Road, which will take you to the Susquehanna River, where there's some parking and an optimum viewing area.

Prepare to be cold because you will be standing around and waiting, with the wind off the water making it even colder. Dress warmly and consider bringing binoculars and a telephoto camera lens. Or

BALD EAGLE MARY HELEN SEAY GRASSO

you can just come to see the bald eagles for yourself. Bring something to eat and drink because there's nothing available for purchase. You might also want to bring a small folding chair; otherwise you're going to be standing a long time.

If it's summertime, there's still a chance to see eagles, though it's less likely. After you've seen as much as you like, head back out and turn left onto US 1 and then make a quick right into the parking lot for the small but excellent visitor center. There you can see photos from some of the photographers' shoots and get information on the dam.

If you're hungry, **Box Hill Pizzeria and Crabcakes** has wonderful—you guessed it—pizza and crabcakes. The vibe is casual, the service is excellent, and it's only a half-hour drive from the dam.

You can head back to Baltimore from the restaurant or the dam.

IN THE AREA

Baltimore City

Accommodations

ADMIRAL FELL INN. Call 410-522-7377. Website: www.admiralfell.com.

KIMPTON HOTEL MONACO BALTIMORE. Call 443-692-6170. Website: www.monaco-baltimore.com.

Activities and Recreation

BROMO SELTZER ARTS TOWER TOUR. Call 443-874-3596. Website: www.bromoseltzertower.com.

EDGAR ALLAN POE GRAVESITE (WESTMINSTER HALL, BURYING GROUNDS, AND CATACOMBS). Call 410-706-2072. Website: www.westminsterhall.org.

M&T BANK STADIUM. Call 410-261-7283. Website: baltimoreravens.com.

ORIOLE PARK AT CAMDEN YARDS. Call 410-685-9800. Website: www.mlb.com/orioles.

WALTERS ART MUSEUM. Call 410-547-9000. Website: www.thewalters.org.

WASHINGTON MONUMENT. Call 410-962-5070. Website: mvpconservancy.org/the-monument.

Dining/Drinks

ALDO'S RISTORANTE ITALIANO. Call 410-727-0700. Website: www.aldositaly.com.

RESTAURANTE TIO PEPE. Call 410-539-4675. Website: www.tiopepe.us.

THE OWL BAR, at the Belvedere. Call 410-347-0888. Website: www.theowlbar.com.

Hunt Valley/Cockeysville

Dining/Drinks

CASA MIA'S RESTAURANT, Parkton. Call 410-357-4231. Website: originalcasamias.com.

PAPPAS RESTAURANT & SPORTS BAR. Call 410-666-0030. Website: pappasrestaurantcockeysville.com.

VITO RISTORANTE ITALIANO. Call 410-666-3100.

Darlington

Activities and Recreation

CONOWINGO DAM.

CONOWINGO VISITOR CENTER. Call 410-457-5011.

RIPKEN STADIUM (ABERDEEN IRONBIRDS). Call 410-297-9292. Website: www.ironbirdsbaseball.com.

Dining/Drinks

BOX HILL PIZZERIA & CRABCAKES, Abingdon. Call 410-515-3662.

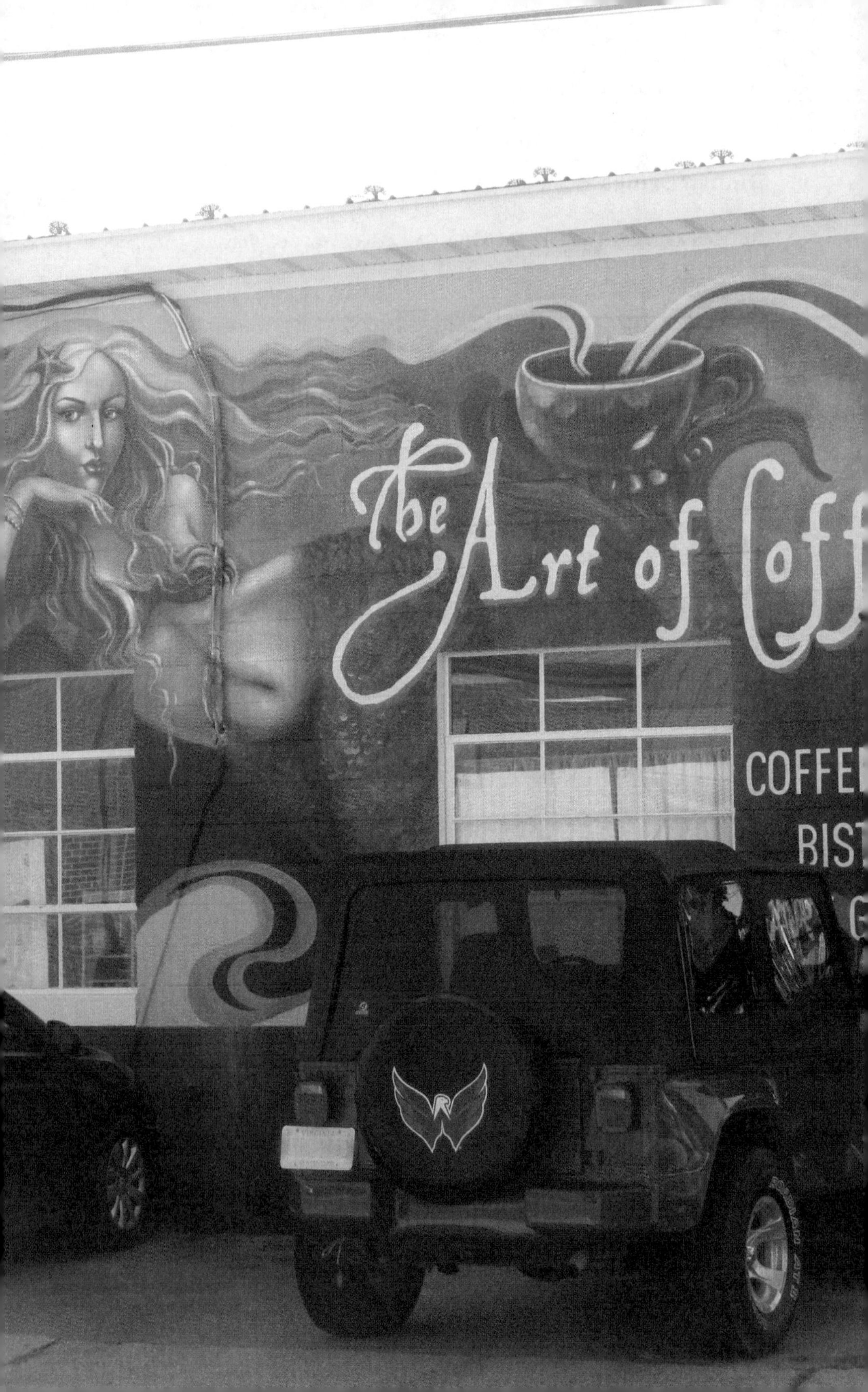
The Art of Coff
COFFE
BIST

17

RELAXING IN VIRGINIA'S NORTHERN NECK

ESTIMATED LENGTH: 200 miles round-trip plus a few nautical miles

ESTIMATED TIME: 3–4 days

GETTING THERE: Take US 301 South from Southern Maryland to the Governor Harry W. Nice Memorial/Senator Thomas "Mac" Middleton Bridge; then cross the Potomac River into the Northern Neck 11.5 miles to VA 3 East. From Richmond, take US 360 East across the Rappahannock River at the Downing Bridge. From Washington, DC, take I-95 South to VA 3 East to the "Neck." By boat, you can also rent a slip at the Tides Inn Marina on Carters Creek, a tributary of the Rappahannock.

HIGHLIGHTS: Outdoor mural art, rural countryside, sailing lessons, sunset boat rides, lovely Tides Inn resort, quirky fun with outdoor chess, bike rides, delicious meals, George Washington's birthplace.

It's called the **Northern Neck** because it's the northernmost Virginia peninsula on the western shore of the Chesapeake Bay. But that's an odd name in the Commonwealth of Virginia, which was at one time the center of the Confederacy—the heart of Southern sentiment in the country. The word "neck" is an old term meaning "peninsula."

Besides the odd nomenclature, this area along the western shore of the Chesapeake Bay is uniquely rural for an area by the bay. It is certainly part of the region, sharing much of the bay's watermen culture. However, it's also different from other parts of the area, for it's not visited as much and not written about as much. Isolation adds to its charm.

Much happened in the Northern Neck, especially in the early years of our nation, for this part of Virginia was home to many of our leaders. After

MURAL OUTSIDE THE ART OF COFFEE IN MONTROSS

all, George Washington's birthplace is in the Northern Neck, as is **Stratford Hall Plantation**, being the birthplace of Robert E. Lee. Both the Washington and Lee families settled in the area, farmed tobacco, and influenced the political course of the nation.

And though it has "northern" in its name, the area is truly southern in nature. Travelers should note that locals refer to the area as "in" the Northern Neck whereas "come-heres" all say "on" the Northern Neck. So if you want to fit in, use "in" rather than "on."

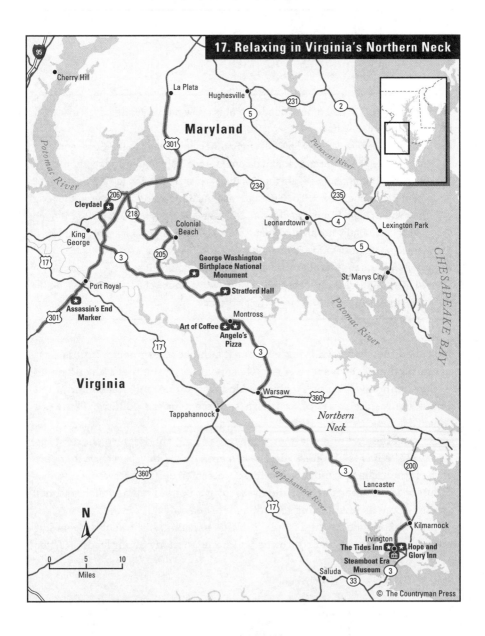

When you first cross onto the peninsula, one of your first stops can be the **George Washington Birthplace National Monument.** The 550-acre property is located at the confluence of the Potomac River and Popes Creek, and it's maintained and operated by the National Park Service. To get there after crossing the Potomac River from the north on US 301, drive about 11.5 miles and turn left onto VA 3 East for another 13 miles. Then take a left onto VA 204 for 2 miles to the park entrance.

Originally a tobacco plantation owned by Washington's great-grandfather, John Washington, the site is bucolic and idyllic. There's a miniature Washington monument close to the entrance and a superb visitor center. If you're traveling with a picnic lunch, you'll easily find a pleasant spot to eat. But don't dawdle because there's so much more to see in the Northern Neck.

Relaxed vibe. With the **Potomac River** to the north, the **Rappahannock River** to the south, and the **Chesapeake Bay** on the east, this area of Virginia is a watermen's haven.

With rural, low density population and relatively deserted roads, it's also an escapist's dream, providing a respite from the crowds and urban life of Washington, DC, to the north and of Norfolk and Richmond to the south. It's a place to wear jeans and flannel shirts, sneakers or boat shoes, and enjoy a beer with your seafood.

Captain John Smith was arguably the area's first tourist. With his crew, he explored and mapped the area during two voyages in 1608. This exploration included contact with the native Algonquian-speaking Indian tribes, including the Rappahannocks.

The tribes hunted, fished, raised crops, and gathered food and raw materials from the land and the waterways. The tribal approach was one of shared natural resources and land use. The colonists were territorial and believed in acquiring property rights, eventually pushing most of the Native Americans out.

Before the Europeans came, the sustainable practices of the Indian tribes preserved the flocks of waterfowl, abundant fish and oysters, and thick forests. Unlike many areas of the Chesapeake, which have changed due to vastly increased populations and development, the Northern Neck is probably closer to those times of abundance due to its sparse population.

In recent years, many Amish families have moved into the area, for the focus on nature and the environment is compatible with their culture. Though traffic is sparse, be cautious when driving, for you may come across a horse-drawn buggy traveling slowly on the same roads.

Outdoor art. Nature is certainly beautiful in this part of the region, but outdoor art is also prevalent, stirring the imagination and sparking interest.

Surprisingly, there are many examples of mural art on the walls of buildings in the Northern Neck. Two towns in particular deserve attention from art lovers and those who enjoy unexpected discovery hidden around corners and on the sides of otherwise ordinary buildings.

Montross is one of the two towns (pronounced *mon-traws*). After visiting Washington's birthplace, continue on VA 3 East into the town and you'll see several murals from the road, including the one outside at **The Art of Coffee**. Inside, another mural is of the Mona Lisa with a cup of coffee. Besides the art, this café is a good place to relax—it's a mellow spot frequented by locals, which is always a good sign.

Montross has a cute streetscape. And it's a good destination for a day or afternoon outing—definitely worth spending a few hours for the adventure of uncovering the various murals in a several block radius.

Colonial Beach is the other art-infused town you'll see toward the end of the trip. It's a good spot to visit on your way home. From the Tides Inn where you'll be staying, travel on VA 3 West to right on VA 205 towards the Potomac River. (To reach Colonial Beach from **Stratford Hall Plantation**, take VA 3 West to VA 205 West into the town.)

Once there, go to the Colonial Beach Municipal Pier and turn left along the beach to see the unique murals on the sides of the men's and women's dressing rooms. And opposite the Riverview Inn on Hawthorn Street is a giant mural of a steamboat.

STEAMBOAT MURAL ON WALL IN COLONIAL BEACH

Creativity in the Public Square

Art provides artists a way to express themselves. This has been going on for thousands of years, beginning with cave dwellers, extending to the great masters and on to modern-day graffiti artists. In urban settings one finds many murals painted on the sides of buildings.

This trend found its way into the rural Northern Neck in two towns—Montross and Colonial Beach—in a big way. Some are in the form of advertising—like on the former Coca-Cola factory in Montross—and most are quirky, entertaining, innovative ways of looking at the setting through an artistic lens.

Paintings are pieces of art on canvas, wood, paper, glass, and other surfaces. A mural is artwork painted directly on a wall, ceiling, or other large permanent type of surface. When done well, the painting complements and is symbiotic with the milieu in which it is set, thus giving context to the work. Often architectural elements of the space and other nearby elements are in harmony with the artist's vision.

In addition to cave paintings found in the south of France and elsewhere, ancient murals have been discovered in Egyptian tombs. And there are Mayan murals dating to 300 BC that were found in Guatemala. In Italy around 1300, artists were fond of painting frescoes on wet plaster, which improved the quality of their murals.

One technique often used is *trompe l'oeil*, which is French for "tricking or fooling the eye." This technique is used to make it seem as if there are doors or windows on a building, for instance, when in fact it is merely a blank wall with realistic-looking doors and windows painted on.

Hand-painted murals are fascinating and bring art to the public square. Their significance and the visual excitement they engender can be invaluable. In Montross and Colonial Beach, if you're not expecting to see art, it can be an astonishing treat.

Even if you know about the existence of these murals in advance, there's still a surprise factor when you turn a corner and actually see one. You can just drive or walk around, enjoying nature and the atmosphere of small-town rural America, while also stimulating a love of, or at least an appreciation for, art.

Where to stay. It's not often that the place we stay is an attraction in and of itself, but in this case that's true. The **Tides Inn** is truly a special place. From the exquisite food to the gorgeous scenery on **Carters Creek**, a tributary of the Rappahannock River, to sailing lessons aboard a lovely boat, this is one place that is not to be missed.

The Tides Inn has been a resort in **Irvington** since 1947. It's a lovely place to enjoy a break. You can learn to sail from a **Premier Sailing** instructor, play nine holes of golf, enjoy the dining, take a short motorboat cruise to watch the sunset over the water, revel in a massage at the spa, or play a game of giant chess on the grounds. You can also use a kayak or paddleboard to explore Carters Creek.

To get to the Tides Inn from Montross on VA 3 East, drive to the town of **Kilmarnock** and take VA 200 South about 5 miles to Irvington. Turn right onto King Carter Drive.

On the way, Kilmarnock is an old-fashioned town with several interesting antiques shops, boutiques, and an art gallery on Main Street. The town park, also on Main Street, has a playground for children and a separate dog park.

Within the Tides Inn resort, the **Chesapeake Restaurant** is superb. You can eat a healthy and delicious breakfast as well as a relaxing and excellent dinner with wine and locally sourced seafood like oysters, rockfish, and crabcakes, plus greens with a Southern bent. To work off the food, there are bicycles you can borrow to explore the grounds and the town of Irvington, a nine-hole golf course where you can practice your swing, and water sports from paddle boarding to sailing.

The Tides Inn is absolutely lovely. But if you want something smaller, another great option in Irvington is the **Hope and Glory Inn.** This small country inn has a charm all its own. Even if you stay at Tides Inn, you may want to have one of the excellent prix fixe dinners at Hope and Glory—reservations required.

For a meal where the locals frequently dine, head back to Montross for lunch or dinner at **Angelo's.** The restaurant serves excellent pizza, pasta, and seafood. It's casual but homey and delicious.

Sailing school. Many of us have long wanted to take sailing lessons. At the Tides Inn you can make that bucket list item a reality with either a beginner or advanced lesson starting from the dock at the Tides Inn Marina. Arabella Denvir is the owner of the **Premier Sailing School**, and she's smart when it comes to teaching sailing, which is certainly in her blood since she hails from a sailing family in Ireland. She came to the "Neck" looking for adventure and never left.

If you don't know a mainsail from a jib or a cleat from a winch handle, you'll soon learn on the little Catalina 27 she may bring to pick you up for your lesson. You'll cast off and manipulate the jib sail in front, which pivots the bow away from the wind.

Normally you can learn to sail in four days over two weekends. But Arabella is accommodating and will happily arrange to give you a three-hour skippered charter to try it out. No doubt it will whet your appetite for more of the sport.

SCENERY WHEN SAILING NEAR TIDES INN

For novices, it's good to know the sheet is a rope controlling a sail. And beware the boom as it swings from side to side. Of course, you can't sail directly into the wind, so you either zigzag or use the motor when heading against the wind.

Once under sail, that magic moment happens that almost everyone loves. With the engine off and quiet, the beauty of being on the water is pervasive and provocative, bringing out a passion for sailing that, once experienced, never totally leaves.

If you're out for an all-day lesson, you'll anchor for lunch and then sail back to the dock in the afternoon. If you chose to merely try sailing for a few hours, you'll be sorry to see the time end.

Civil War. One of the more riveting stories in American history, as if it was not enough that it was a significant moment that forever changed the psyche of the country, is the assassination of Abraham Lincoln and the subsequent escape of, and dramatic hunt for, John Wilkes Booth through the Maryland and Virginia countrysides.

While Ford's Theatre in Washington, DC, has an elaborate exhibit dedicated to the story, and tours take place along the Maryland hideouts of the assassin and his accomplices, Virginia is quieter about the story. Perhaps because Virginians lost the war, perhaps because the assassination further infuriated the Union victors, or perhaps because they just wanted to put

CLEYDAEL WHERE BOOTH SOUGHT, AND WAS REFUSED, REFUGE

down their arms and return to life outside combat and hardship, Booth was, in many ways, *persona non grata* in Virginia.

No major battle took place in the Northern Neck, due to the lack of roads and a multitude of waterways large and small. Thus, it's exciting to uncover remnants of Booth's final journey on the south side of the Potomac River.

Booth escaped in a small vessel on his second try across the Potomac from Maryland. Then he sought refuge and medical attention at Dr. Richard Stuart's home, Cleydael, in the Northern Neck. However, Stuart knew of the assassination and was wary of his visitors, so he sent them away after feeding Booth and David Herold, one of Booth's accomplices.

NEAR SITE WHERE BOOTH SOUGHT ASSISTANCE

To see the house at Cleydael from US 301, take VA 206 (Dahlgren Road) West to left on Cleydael Boulevard then right onto Peppermill Road. The house is on the right at 7144. Built in 1859, Cleydael is an impressive farmhouse with a long driveway and circular turnaround.

Booth and Herold then crossed the Rappahannock River. To see where they landed, from Cleydael go left onto VA 206 West to left on VA 611 to right onto US 301 South. Cross the Rappahannock on the James Madison Memorial Bridge. Take the first left onto Water Street in the town of Port Royal, then another left onto King Street to the fishing pier at the end. There's a sign on your right about Booth's landing there.

Next, backtrack on King Street to Water Street, and cross the northbound lane of US 301, taking a left onto US 301 South. Turn around by making a U-turn near US Army Garrison Fort A.P. Hill just north of Bowling Green, and head back north on US 301. On this north side of the split highway is a sign marking the location of the farm where Booth was killed when Union soldiers discovered he was hiding in a barn.

The original roadside marker was erected in 1937 and stolen in 2014. In 2015, a new sign was erected on northbound US 301 around 2 miles south of Port Royal. Marking the location where US cavalrymen captured and mortally wounded Booth, the sign reads, "Assassin's End."

Before or after tracking Booth's last movements, you can go to **Stratford Hall Plantation** to see where General Robert E. Lee was born. The Georgian-style Great House and former plantation long predate the Civil War, but of course, Lee was one of the war's central figures. Stratford Hall is between Montross and Colonial Beach. To reach Stratford, take US 301 North to VA 3 East to VA 214 (Stratford Hall Road).

WHERE MANHUNT FOR JOHN WILKES BOOTH ENDED

Steamboat era. Like on the Eastern Shore, the advent of steamboat routes across the bay and into the Northern Neck were vital to the area's development.

In Irvington, just a few miles from Tides Inn, the **Steamboat Era Museum** at 156 King Carter Drive beautifully documents and illustrates the story of the steamboats and how they impacted lives on the Chesapeake Bay. After all, this mode of transportation provided an economic lifeline from rural villages in the Neck to Norfolk and Baltimore during the era from 1870 to 1925. The cities had markets and the towns had goods to sell, with steamboats providing transportation between the two.

The wharves in the towns were the center of commerce, travel, and social life. And when the steamboats arrived, they blew their distinctive whistles, exciting the local populace who came running to hear the latest news and greet visitors. Commerce went both ways, with local oystermen selling their catch and farmers their produce, while local residents would buy all kinds of manufactured and canned goods.

Many small-town museums are of limited interest to visitors, especially when we're spoiled with world-class repositories in our major cities. But it's definitely worth a visit to this charming museum if this romantic mode of travel interests you at all.

Check in advance for hours based on the season, because the museum is closed in winter and open only limited days during the rest of the year. If you can make the scheduling work, this museum should be a must.

Just like in Maryland, there was a whole network of steamboats servicing this part of Virginia and running from Baltimore to Norfolk and many towns and villages in-between.

The steamboats fostered the expansion of travel and trade—the movement of supplies and people. And these boats carried mail besides their cargo and passengers. It was through these vessels that rural communities became connected to the big cities. Irvington had one of these wharves. So did most other towns and villages in the Northern Neck, including Reedville, Kinsale, and Colonial Beach. If a place was on the water, it almost always had a steamboat landing—the true ticket to isolation back then was not to have one.

Whether you tour around the "Neck" or stay put in a small part of the area, after enjoying the relative isolation and the water you find at nearly every turn, you'll remember this trip fondly and will no doubt want to return.

IN THE AREA

Colonial Beach

Attractions and Recreation

GEORGE WASHINGTON BIRTHPLACE NATIONAL MONUMENT. Call 804-224-1732, ext. 227. Website: www.nps.gov/gewa.

MURAL ART THROUGHOUT TOWN, especially along Hawthorn Street, Colonial Avenue, and Taylor Street.

Irvington

Accommodations

HOPE AND GLORY INN. Call 804-438-6053. Website: hopeandglory.com.

TIDES INN. Call 804-438-5000 or 877-665-5977 (reservations). Website: tidesinn.com.

Attractions and Recreation

STEAMBOAT ERA MUSEUM. Call 804-438-6888. Website: steamboatera museum.org.

Kilmarnock

Attractions and Recreation

ANTIQUES SHOPS, on Main Street and School Street.

Montross

Attractions and Recreation

MURAL ART THROUGHOUT TOWN.

STRATFORD HALL PLANTATION (ROBERT E. LEE'S BIRTHPLACE). Call 804-493-8038. Website: stratfordhall.org.

Dining/Drinks

ANGELO'S RESTAURANT & RAW BAR. Call 804-493-8694.

THE ART OF COFFEE (ART GALLERY AND EATERY). Call 804-493-9651. Website: theartofcoffee.biz.

Port Royal

Attractions and Recreation

JOHN WILKES BOOTH SIGNAGE.

Resources for Further Information

DELAWARE

Delaware Tourism. Call 1-866-284-7483. Website: www.visitdelaware.com.

Greater Wilmington Convention & Visitor Bureau. Call 1-800-489-6664. Website: www.visitwilmingtonde.com.

Kent County Tourism. Call 302-734-4888. Website: www.visitdover.com.

Southern Delaware Tourism. Call 302-856-1818 or 1-800-357-1818. Website: www.visitsoutherndelaware.com.

MARYLAND

Calvert County Department of Economic Development. Call 410-535-1600. Website: www.co.cal.md.us.

Caroline County Office of Tourism. Call 410-479-0655. Website: www.tourcaroline.com.

Cecil County Office of Economic Development & Tourism. Call 1-800-232-4595. Website: www.seececil.org.

Chesapeake Bay Bridge. Call 1-877-229-7726. Website: www.baybridge.maryland.gov.

Dorchester County Tourism. Call 410-228-1000. Website: www.visitdorchester.org.

Kent County Office of Tourism. Call 410-778-0416. Website: www.kentcounty.com.

Maryland Office of Tourism. Call 1-866-639-3526. Website: www
.visitmaryland.org.

Ocean City Department of Tourism. Call 1-800-626-2326. Website: www
.ococean.com.

Queen Anne's County Tourism Office. Call 410-604-2100. Website: www
.visitqueenannes.com.

Somerset County Tourism. Call 410-651-2968 or 1-800-521-9189. Website:
www.visitsomerset.com.

Talbot County Office of Tourism, Easton. Call 410-770-8000. Website:
www.tourtalbot.org.

Visit Baltimore. Call 410-659-7300 or 1-877-225-8466. Website: www
.baltimore.org.

Wicomico County Tourism. Call 1-800-332-8687. Website: www
.wicomicotourism.org.

Worcester County Tourism. Call 410-632-3110 or 1-800-852-0335. Website: www.visitworcester.org.

NEW JERSEY

Chamber of Commerce of Greater Cape May. Call 609-884-5508. Website: www.capemaychamber.com.

Delaware River and Bay Authority (Cape May–Lewes Ferry). Call 1-800-
643-3779. Website: www.drba.net.

Mid-Atlantic Center for the Arts & Humanities (Cape May). Call 609-
884-5404 or 1-800-275-4278. Website: www.capemaymac.org.

PENNSYLVANIA

Chester County Conference and Visitor Bureau (Brandywine Valley).
Call 484-770-8550. Website: www.brandywinevalley.com.

VIRGINIA

Chesapeake Bay Bridge-Tunnel. Call 757-331-2960. Website: www.cbbt
.com.

Eastern Shore of Virginia Tourism. Call 757-787-8268. Website: www
.esvatourism.org.

Northern Neck Tourism Commission. Call 804-333-1919. Website: www.northernneck.org.

Virginia Tourism Corporation. Call 804-545-5600. Website: www.virginia.org.

Acknowledgments

Many thanks to those friends who encourage me to follow my heart's desire wherever my passions lead me and who embrace my penchant for exploration and perpetual curiosity.

Special thanks to the many people who went above and beyond. Your assistance was invaluable in creating this book: Paige Addison, Joyce Baki, Teresa Ballard, Brent Burkhardt, Tina Coleman, Danielle Emerson, Amanda Fenstermaker, Pam George, Mary Helen Grasso, Lisa Hull, Tracey Johns, Danielle Jonigan, Nina Kelly, Christina Lippincott, Heather Taylor, Scott Thomas, Mary Tilghman, and Sandy Turner, among many others.

And to the many generous people I continually meet on my travels, thank you for sharing yourselves and your love of special places.

OSPREY NEST ON PILINGS OFF CHINCOTEAGUE

Index